Eldon Moran

The reporting style of short-hand.

A complete textbook of American phonography. To which is added a series of lessons on amanuensis, speech, legislative, and law reporting

Eldon Moran

The reporting style of short-hand.
A complete textbook of American phonography. To which is added a series of lessons on amanuensis, speech, legislative, and law reporting

ISBN/EAN: 9783337717261

Printed in Europe, USA, Canada, Australia, Japan

Cover: Foto ©ninafisch / pixelio.de

More available books at **www.hansebooks.com**

THE
REPORTING STYLE

OF

SHORT-HAND.

A COMPLETE TEXT-BOOK OF AMERICAN PHONOGRAPHY.

TO WHICH IS ADDED

A SERIES OF LESSONS ON AMANUENSIS, SPEECH, LEGISLATIVE, AND LAW REPORTING.

By ELDON MORAN,

PRINCIPAL INSTRUCTOR STATE UNIVERSITY OF IOWA SCHOOL OF SHORT-HAND, AND LATE OFFICIAL STENOGRAPHER FOR THE COURTS AT INDIANAPOLIS, IND.

DESIGNED FOR USE IN SCHOOLS AND COLLEGES, AND IN CONNECTION WITH THE AUTHOR'S PERFECTED METHOD OF POSTAL INSTRUCTION.

FIFTH EDITION.

ST. LOUIS:
CHRISTIAN PUBLISHING COMPANY.
1887.

COPYRIGHT, 1884,
BY ELDON MORAN.

ALL RIGHTS RESERVED.

PREFACE.

To impart practical instruction in the Reporting Style of the American Pitman Phonography, the system now employed by most professional reporters, is the aim of this work. The Corresponding Style, which cannot be made a substitute for long-hand, and serves no end not better met by the briefer method, is for these reasons discarded. Heretofore the only accessible way to the Reporting Style has been through the Corresponding, a circuitous route, requiring much needless time and labor. This treatise is designed as a school and college text-book, and is well adapted to self-instruction. It is also the basis of the Author's mode of teaching by mail, known as the Perfected Method of Postal Stenography. The best results of his twelve years experience as verbatim reporter and teacher are embraced herein. Printed in separate sheets, these lessons have been used for the past three years in giving instruction to large classes in the State University of Iowa School of Short-Hand. The advantages of omitting the Corresponding Style, and requiring speed in writing from the first, have been fully demonstrated in this Institution, students in some instances having taken secretaryships in eleven weeks from the date of entry. The names of a few of the stenographers who became qualified in this way will be found at the close of the book.

An important feature is the series of lessons on professional reporting, nothing similar to which is to be found in any other instruction book whatever. These explain the forms and methods made use of in amanuensis, convention, legislative, and law reporting, without a knowledge of which the art is quite unavailable as a business. A vocabulary of all the word and phrase signs in common use is appended. Those who have not the assistance of a teacher, and are desirous of progressing rapidly, will be enabled to do so by procuring instruction by mail. The first lessons are furnished gratuitously to those wishing to test the efficiency of this method.

To all those young men and women who have the courage to undertake, and perseverance to master this truly beautiful art, the present work is inscribed with the sincere wish that it may render them genuine service.

Finally, to his kind assistants, by whose careful labors he has profited much, are tendered the grateful acknowledgments of

THE AUTHOR.

Stenographic Supply Agency,
Iowa City, Ia., September, 1887.

NOTE TO THE FOURTH EDITION.

A number of brief paragraphs, containing practical hints and directions, are added to several of the lessons in this edition. The portions quoted are taken from a recent work, entitled, "One Hundred Valuable Suggestions to Short-hand Students," by Selby A. Moran, of the Stenographic Institute, Michigan University.   E. M.

August, 1886.

CONTENTS.

LESSON.		PAGE.
	INTRODUCTION	7
I.	CONSONANT ALPHABET—1ST SEC.	15
II.	" " 2ND SEC.	18
III.	WORD-SIGNS	20
IV.	RAY, AND PHRASEOGRAPHY	24
V.	LONG VOWELS	28
VI.	DIPHTHONGS AND THE S-CIRCLE	33
VII.	SHORT VOWELS	37
VIII.	CONSONANT POSITION	41
IX.	S-CIRCLE JUNCTIONS	45
X.	PHRASEOGRAPHY	48
XI.	SEZ-CIRCLE, EMP, AND COALESCENTS	51
XII.	DOUBLE CONSONANTS—THE L-HOOK	55
XIII.	THE R-HOOK SERIES—1ST SEC.	59
XIV.	" " " 2ND SEC.	63
XV.	TRIPLE CONSONANTS	66
XVI.	THE REL-HOOK, AND THE ASPIRATE TICK AND DOT	69
XVII.	THE W-HOOK	71
XVIII.	THE F-HOOK	74
XIX.	THE N-HOOK SERIES—1ST SEC.	77
XX.	" " " 2ND SEC.	79
XXI.	THE SHUN-HOOK	82
XXII.	THE S-SHUN AND INITIAL N HOOKS	85
XXIII.	THE ST AND STR LOOPS.	88

CONTENTS.

LESSON.		PAGE
XXIV.	The Lengthened Curve	91
XXV.	The Halving Principle	93
XXVI.	" " " Added D	96
XXVII.	" " " Shortened Double Consonants	100
XXVIII.	The Halving Principle—Shortened Final-Hook Consonants	103
XXIX.	The Halving Principle—Shortened Liquids	107
XXX.	Intervocalization	110
XXXI.	Prefixes	113
XXXII.	Affixes	117
XXXIII.	Expedients and Punctuation	119
XXXIV.	General Principles	122
XXXV.	Proper Names	125
XXXVI.	Special Rules	127
XXXVII.	Amanuensis Reporting	130
XXXVIII.	" " Continued	134
XXXIX.	Speech Reporting	139
XL.	Convention Reporting	143
XLI.	Law Reporting—Caption, Question and Answer	148
XLII.	Law Reporting—Objections, Rulings, and Exceptions	153
XLIII.	Law Reporting—Exhibits and Indices	159
XLIV.	" " Transcripts	165
XLV.	" " Professional Conduct	170
Suggestions		176
Vocabulary		177
Verbatim Reporting Speed		185
Note to the Third Edition		187
Commendations		188

INTRODUCTION.

This Science is still much younger than many of its practitioners. The advancement made in a few decades is truly astonishing. But years of experiment and elaboration are still needed to thoroughly unify and complete the system. The physician's art, old as the race, continues to be enriched by discoveries, and the methods of instruction in its principles improved by the enlargement of hospitals, the increase of clinical facilities, and the publication of better illustrated and more methodic text books. But scientific shorthand is only in its infancy, and it would be sheer folly to disregard the suggestions of the ingenious minds assiduously at work in every corner of this field. The standard systems, so called, which admit of no modification, are fast falling into disuse. The notion given out by some, that further improvement is impossible or useless, is absurd. Development gradually goes on, and the method of teaching has been so far perfected that the skill which once demanded two years to gain, may now be acquired in four months.

The method of instruction here employed is practical and progressive. The principles of the system are taken up and explained in logical order, and the student directed how to apply them correctly in the work of forming the characters rapidly and artistically. Two or three new principles only are introduced in a single lesson, and a list of words inserted which are to be written in accordance therewith. The words chosen for this purpose are those in common use. The drill which enables the student to write and read them with the required speed, fixes the characters firmly in his memory. This makes an extended vocabulary unnecessary, since an outline, once well learned, will be remembered. No word or phrase is introduced which the learner has not been fully directed how to write in the proper manner. It is a loss instead of gain to practice writing words not found in the regular lists, since in most cases the outlines will necessarily be formed incorrectly. The disadvantage of attempting words too soon may be illustrated by an engraving of the characters produced by successive trial to write September:

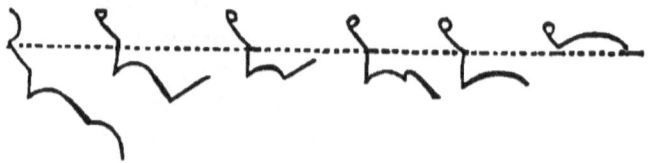

When two lessons only are learned, the first character will be produced; when six lessons are learned, the second character; eleven lessons, the third; thirteen lessons, the fourth; twenty-four lessons, the fifth; and twenty-five lessons, the sixth. The last only is correct. The practice of representing this word by five different and erroneous outlines, makes it the more difficult afterwards to impress the right one upon the mind; and when the word is to be written, the reporter is confused and bewildered by the jumble of forms his recollection calls up. It has been the aim in preparing this work to entirely do away all cause for the criticism justly passed on other instruction books, that words and phrases were introduced merely for the student's practice, and written in a dozen erroneous ways before the proper outlines were taught.

The Reporting Field. Although this art was originally devised as a means of preserving, word for word, the speeches of great orators, and the proceedings of legislatures and courts, it has been found far more valuable as a means of expediting commercial transactions. While the services of an expert reporter are always in demand, there are at present more frequent calls for secretaries who are able to write with a moderate degree of speed only. The verbatim stenographer must be able to write one hundred and seventy-five to two hundred words a minute, and it is his business to report speeches, and record the proceedings of courts and the various kinds of public assemblies. His annual income ranges from one to four thousand dollars. Short-hand secretaries are employed by all kinds of business houses, companies, and corporations; also, by authors, ministers, lawyers, and professional men generally. Amanuenses must be able to write one hundred to one hundred and fifty words a minute; and they receive as compensation from sixty to one hundred and fifty dollars a month. Ladies are frequently employed in this capacity. There is a large and ever increasing demand for skilled short-hand writers. They succeed best who are gifted with mental quickness, and who have good memories, the kind especially which enables them to recognize old faces. These faculties, with perseverance, will enable any intelligent young person to acquire skill enough in a few months for amanuensis work.

Experience shows that this art can be successfully learned by both old and young. Those receiving instruction at the University School of Short-hand range in age from twelve to fifty.

Students who wish to perfect themselves in the shortest time possible, may do so by applying to the author, who will furnish personal instruction by mail, and assist them, when competent, in obtaining situations.

Short-hand is not only valuable as a profession; it is equally useful as an accomplishment. No thinking man can afford to be without this rapid method of transferring his thoughts to paper. By means of it, first draughts of letters and articles are made, and notes of lectures, business transactions, and private memoranda recorded, much more fully and in but a fraction of the time otherwise required. Its great utility, both as a discipline and personal convenience, is abundantly attested by literary men of note who are skilled in its use.

The learner must bear in mind at the outset, that short-hand is something *practical*, and that no matter how carefully the *theory* is studied, he will gain but little proficiency if he does not at the same time learn to form the characters quickly and well, and read his notes fluently. The common method of learning all the principles before any effort is made at rapid writing, is but a waste of time. It is more difficult to *execute* than to *memorize* the characters; hence, directions as to the work of *getting up speed* are given early in the course. Those who intend making this art a business, should practice upon each exercise until it can be written in the time specified. The skill gained in this way will be sufficient for ordinary amanuensis work. Some will rise above, and others, especially if under sixteen, will necessarily fall below the speed here indicated.

Reading Practice. The amount of this that may be necessary will depend on yourself. If you read your own writing with difficulty, you should practice only so much the more. Those who employ their time mainly in writing, with a view of gaining speed, producing inaccurate and misshapen characters which they rarely attempt to read, may rest assured that they are making progress backward instead of forward. When all the list words of a single lesson have been carefully written, they should then be read over and over again, until the whole can be rendered in the time indicated by the following table:

LESSON	I.—1m.	LESSON	XII.—1½m.	LESSON	XXIII.—2m.
"	II.—1m.	"	XIII.—5m.	"	XXIV.—1m.
"	III.—3m.	"	XIV.—2½m.	"	XXV.—4m.
"	IV.—2m.	"	XV.—1½m.	"	XXVI.—5m.
"	V.—5m.	"	XVI.—2m.	"	XXVII.—3m.
"	VI.—6m.	"	XVII.—½m.	"	XXVIII.—4½m.
"	VII.—4m.	"	XVIII.—¾m.	"	XXIX.—½m.
"	VIII.—3m.	"	XIX.—3m.	"	XXX.—4m.
"	IX.—3m.	"	XX.—3½m.	"	XXXI.—5m.
"	X.—2m.	"	XXI.—4m.	"	XXXII.—½m.
"	XI.—2½m.	"	XXII.—1½m.		

LONG AND SHORT HAND COMPARED.

One is written six times faster than the other; and there are six general principles by which the common method of writing is abbreviated, six steps, so to speak, in the ladder leading from the long up to the short-hand system.

I. *A letter for a sound.* In *dough* but two sounds are heard, those of *d* and *o*; nevertheless five letters, *d-o-u-g-h*, are employed to express them. In short-hand but two letters are required, one for each sound, thus |— *dough*.

II. *A single stroke for a letter.* The long-hand *d* is written with five strokes of the pen, while the short-hand | *d* requires but one; the long-hand *o* requires four strokes, the short-hand — *o* but one.

III. *Omission of vowels.* In short-hand, much less than one per cent. of the vowels are actually written, but a number sufficient to secure legibility are *indicated* by the manner of writing the consonant signs. The consonant elements of a word may be expressed by several different outlines, the particular one selected being determined by the number of vowels contained, and the order in which they occur. Hence, in reading short-hand, it becomes an easy matter to supply those vowels upon which the choice of the characters made use of directly depended. Each of the following characters, for example, express the consonants *s-p-r-t*, being the same which occur in the corresponding words:

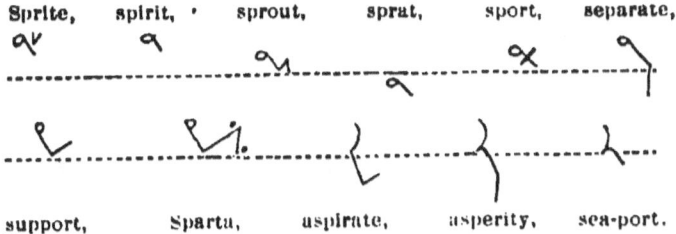

In *sprite, sprout, sport,* and *Sparta,* the vowels are written. *Spirit* and *sprat,* although written alike, are distinguished by the positions which they occupy with reference to the base line. The characters for the remaining words all differ from each other, the particular outline chosen in each case indicating the number and position of vowels to be supplied. Thus each character is rendered legible, although the consonants only are actually written. This principle may be illustrated in part by omitting the vowels from a printed sentence, which will nevertheless be found easily decipherable: G-d s- -d l-t th-r- b- l-ght, -nd th-r- w-s l-ght.

IV. *The use of brief word signs.* A large number of abbreviations are used in long-hand, as *Dec., Ib., &, Dr., U. S., Hon.,* etc. Likewise in short-hand, brief characters, called *word-signs,* are employed; e. g. *which* is signified by the sign for , *eh* simply, *think* by the sign for (*th*, etc. These short-hand signs are provided for the most frequently recurring words only, as ⌐ *have,* ₁ *before,* ⌐ *will,* ⌐ *thing,* *has,* and ⌐ *what,* which is not true of long-hand abbreviations.

V. *Phraseography, or joining words together.* In long-hand, the pen is lifted from the paper upon the completion of each word. In short-hand, from three to ten words are written before this is necessary; *e. g.*:

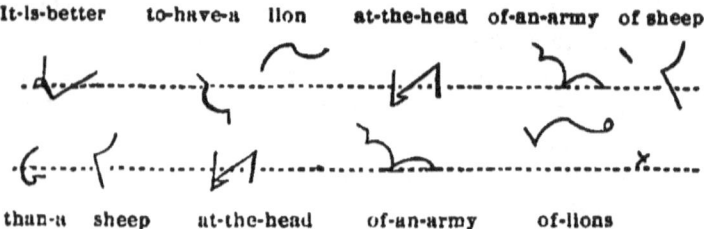

VI. *The use of expedients.* The most frequently recurring phrases are represented by brief signs which express two or more of the principal words of each, thus:

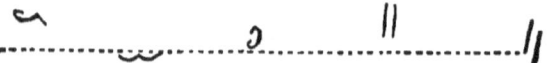

In-order-to, hand-in-hand, on-the-other-hand, from-time-to-time, day-after-day.

GENERAL DIRECTIONS.

1. Hold your pen in a position very nearly upright.
2. Always write on ruled paper.
3. Use a short-nibbed pen with moderately sharp point. Gillott, Nos. 303 and 404 the Esterbrook school pen, and some Nos. of the Spencerian, are recommended. The pen with which you can produce the most satisfactory work is the one best suited to your hand and style of writing. Jet black, easily flowing ink should be used, and the bottle kept corked. Carter's koal black ink is recommended.
4. Read over at least once everything you write.
5. Do not allow a day to pass without devoting some time to practice, if only a few minutes.
6. Rigidly abstain from practicing on words and sentences not found in the lessons which have been learned.
7. It is very important that you write the exercises as they are distinctly read to you. A fellow student, who has an interest in the work himself, will generally prove most serviceable for this purpose. The habit of writing by sound, that is, recording words that are

heard rather than merely *seen*, is simply indispensable to the student who intends using short-hand for reporting purposes.

8. About one-third of the time set apart for reading should be spent in translating exercises written one or two weeks previously.

9. In writing an exercise for the first time you should form the characters slowly. When you have executed the whole in a proper manner, copy it over and over again until you can write it at the specified rate of speed.

10. The learner cannot become too familiar with the manner of writing the words given in these lists, as they are always expressed by the same characters which here denote them. The word and phrase signs given in the vocabulary should be thoroughly learned.

11. The student should give especial attention to phraseography, as this important part of the system is often neglected.

12. Beginners commonly write the characters too large. The standard, one-sixth of an inch, should be as closely adhered to as possible. This size of writing can best be secured by making use of stenographic practice books such as are supplied by the Reporters' Bureau.

13. When practicing, the note-book or paper should be held firm by placing the thumb and first fingers of the left hand one or two inches above the line of writing.

14. After thirty-six lessons are learned the student's practice need not be limited to the exercises here given, but easy newspaper articles, the prose part of school readers, printed collections of business letters, and published reports of law and convention proceedings, may be profitably used for this purpose. Great care should be taken to write each article properly the first time, and to rewrite it afterwards not less than three or four times with gradually increased speed.

15. Carry a list of word and phrase signs, and a copy of your last written exercise, in your pocket, to read over and memorize at leisure moments.

16. In making memoranda, or in corresponding with those who understand them, you should employ the short-hand characters as fast as learned.

17. You will find the study more interesting, and progress faster,

by having a fellow student with whom to meet at stated times for practice.

18. Not only can a more lively interest in the work be kept up, but real advantage is gained, by students corresponding with each other in the stenographic characters. The author, when applied to, will be pleased to introduce those wishing to enter into such an arrangement

.

DEFINITION OF TERMS.

Stenography.—A system of rapid writing; Short-hand.

Phonography.—Sound-writing; a phonetic system of Short-hand.

Word-Sign.—An abbreviated outline in which some of the consonants are omitted.

Sign-Word.—A word which is provided with a sign, or abbreviated outline.

Phraseograph.—A character expressing more words than one, formed by writing a number of words without lifting the pen.

Phrase-Sign.—An abbreviated phraseograph.

Phraseogram.—An assemblage of words which are expressed by a phrase-sign.

Consonant Stem.—Any letter of the consonant alphabet, whether standard length, shortened or lengthened.

Adjunctive Sign.—Any character or expedient, other than the letters of the alphabet, which is employed to express a consonant sound; *e. g.*, the s-circle, n-hook, st-loop, cmp, etc.

Verbatim.—Word for word.

Notes.—Matter written in Short-hand; Stenographic manuscript.

List-Words.—Series of words to be written according to the rules which just precede them. The list-words of some lessons are distributed into several paragraphs; *e. g.*, see lesson XI, sections 164, 166, 169, and 171.

Speed Sentence.—The sentence which is to be written a given number of times in so many minutes; *e. g.*, see sec. 270.

NOTE.—The attention of the student is called to the explanation of our method of giving lessons by mail and of instructing correspondence classes, found at the close of the book.

THE REPORTING STYLE OF SHORT-HAND.

LESSON I.

CONSONANT ALPHABET, SEC. 1.

1.

1. pe	\	pit, lip.	5. chay	/	choice, each.
2. be	\	boat, tub.	6. jay	/	joy, gem, edge.
3. te	|	top, mat.	7. kay	—	kite, lack.
4. de	|	do, sad.	8. gay	—	go, log.

2. Each of the short-hand letters here given represents an elementary consonant sound, and has a force equivalent to the full-faced type in the corresponding words. Each is to be used *whenever*, and *only when*, its particular *sound* is *heard*. The character \ pe, for example, signifies the breath sound of *p* in *pie* or *ape*, and is employed only when this occurs. It will be observed, however, that this sound does not recur as frequently as the common or long-hand *p*. In *sophist*, for example, this element is not found, the long-hand *p* being taken with *h* to represent the force of *f*. In *copper*, this sound occurs but once, the first *p* being used merely to indicate that *o* is short.

3. In sound-writing, only as many letters are employed as there are distinct sounds heard; thus *fo*, foe, *na*, nay; *lo*, low; *felo*, fellow; *do*, dough; *fabl*, fable; *fonograf*, phonograph; *mikst*, mixed; *kwil*, quill; *hwen*, when. There are no silent letters, as *b* in lamb; no unnecessary letters, as *x* and *c*, which could be dispensed with, *x* having the force as *ks*, as in tax, or of *gz*, as in example, and *c* that commonly of either *s*, as in face, or *k*, as in come; sometimes of *sh*, as in vicious. Hence the usual manner of spelling a word has *nothing whatever* to do in determining the way in which it is written in short-hand.

4. The characters which express the consonant sounds of a word, when written in the order in which they occur, are called its *consonant delineation*. For example, for *take*, te-kay is the delineation; for *jug*, jay-gay; for *keg*, kay-gay; etc.

5. These, when joined or written together, are called a *consonant outline*, as in *betake*, or *digit*. This should be executed without lifting the pen from the paper, each successive letter being written in its proper direction, beginning where the preceding ends, thus,

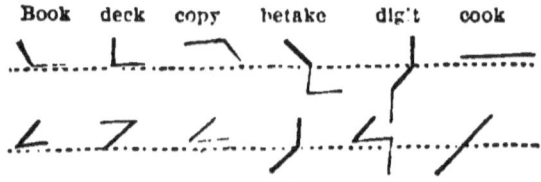

6. The rule for placing outlines is that the *first descending letter should rest on the line*. This requires that some letters be written one space above, as ¯ kay in *copy*, which is necessary in this case, in order that ⸜ pe, the first downward letter, may rest upon it.

7. Write each letter longer or shorter with reference to a fixed standard, which should not vary much from the sixth of an inch. Assuming te to be the standard, all other vertical letters should be the same height. Kay, also, should be the same length, and other horizontal consonants should occupy an equal space along the line. All slanting letters are written the same height as te, their length depending on the degree of inclination.

8. The side of a square in the stenographic practice book is one sixth of an inch. The proper length for letters is secured by writing each only as long as the square will allow, as shown by the figure:

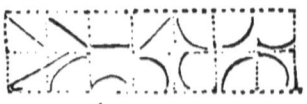

9. Caution.—The student is apt, at first, to incline te and de somewhat to the right, and to give too little slant to inclined letters. This fault may be overcome by writing te, and other upright letters, so as to correspond with the vertical lines in the practice book; also, by writing pe, chay, and other slanting letters in such a manner as to extend diagonally across the square.

10. The first six letters are always written downward; but horizontal letters, as ⸺ kay and ⸺ gay, are executed from left to right.

11. Give each letter its proper attitude, as follows: | te and | de, vertical; \ pe and \ be, right slant; / chay and / jay, left slant, at an angle of forty-five degrees with the horizontal. Care should be taken to make the light letters thin as possible, and the heavy ones thick enough only to be readily distinguished from the light.

12. Each letter, when standing alone, should rest on the line.

13. The pen should be held between the thumb and first and second fingers, not far from the nib, and in a nearly upright position, as shown in the first figure. The practical stenographer will, however, derive rest from an occasional change to the position shown in the second figure.

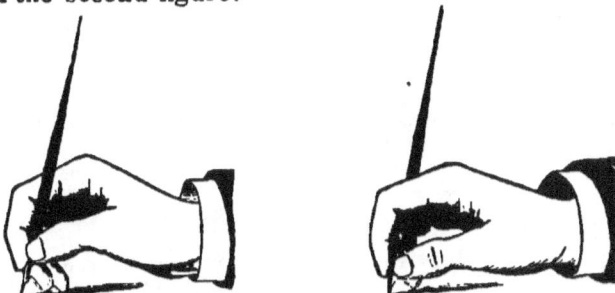

14. Copy Sec. 1 of the alphabet forty to fifty times, or until you can make every character accurately soon as read to you.

15. The student will observe that several different words may have the same outline, as te-kay for both take and took, gay-de for guide and giddy, be-gay for big and beg. But this is merely accidental, and no ambiguity results from it. In the sentence, for instance, "Those \⸺ boys \⸺ bread" the context enables the reader to determine when this character signifies *big* and when *beg*. Here be-gay denotes first an adjective, then a verb; and it is a rule that the same character may represent two or more different parts of speech without danger of ambiguity.

EXERCISE 1.

16. Write the consonant outlines for the following words: Take, deck, pick, check, keep, took, deep, guide, dog, jug, do, pay, up, it, be, go, cage, ditch, pig, budge, dodge, pitch, judge, page, betake, bedeck, touch, copy, pity, abate, abode, giddy, body, edit, book, deputy, jacket, pocket, bucket, ducat. (Twice in 3 min.)

LESSON II.

CONSONANT ALPHABET, SEC. 2.

17. 9. ef — fan, laugh, physic.
10. ve — vine, love.
11. ith — think, both.
12. the — them, soothe.
13. es — so, face.
14. ze — zeal, was.
15. ish — shall, vicious.
16. zhe — seizure, pleasure.
17. lay — light, bell.
18. ar — arm, furrow.
19. em — me, him.
20. en — no, in.
21. ing — ing, ink.
22. way — woe, away.
23. yea — your.
24. hay — he.

18. Table showing directions in which all the alphabetic letters are to be written:

Downward:

To the right: ⸺ ⸺ ⌒ ⌣ ⌣ ;   Upward:

19. Straight letters should be made without crook or curvature. Curves should be bent uniformly throughout, and the thickened ones allowed to taper at the extremities.

20. The student should spend at least fifteen minutes a day for one or two weeks in the oral outlining of words. Beginning with any list found in this book, first pronounce the word aloud, and then name the letters in the order, which, if written, would constitute its consonant delineation. Thus, *system* would be spelled, es-es-te-em; *short-hand*, ish-ar-te-hay-en-de; *stenography*, es-te-en-gay-ar-ef; *tax*, te-kay-es; *example*, gay-ze-em-pe-lay; *quill*, kay-way-lay; *white*, hay-way-te; *erasure*, ar-zhe-ar.

21. Short-hand is very different from a mere abbreviated long-hand. In writing it you should not attempt to spell out words, as you do in long-hand, but simply write the consonant sounds that are actually heard. In lodge (lay-jay), for example, there is no de; in bell (be-lay), there is but one lay; in arrow, but one ar. Final *y* is never yea, but always a vowel. (Vowels will be explained in a subsequent lesson.)

22. In common long-hand an elementary sound is sometimes represented by one letter and sometimes by another; as, for example, the force of f is also given to ph. But in short-hand each distinct sound is provided with a separate character, which always denotes that particular sound, and can never denote any other.

23. The perfect adaptation of the written characters to the sounds which they express is shown in part by the following examples: The two similar and cognate sounds, \ pe and \ be, are denoted by two similar characters, the aspirate pe being appropriately expressed by a light, and the subvocal be by a shaded, stroke. Be differs from pe only in point of shade, which is sufficient distinction, since, should pe be shaded too much, or be too little, no uncertainty of meaning would result; *e. g.*, the sentence, "It is pest to bay as you go," is of no doubtful signification. The same principle applies in the case of each other pair of cognates: te and de, kay and gay, ef and ve, etc. Also, observe that the explodents are appropriately expressed by straight letters, while the continuents and liquids are indicated by curves.

24. Copy Sec. 2 of the alphabet many times, until you can write all the characters readily at dictation. Then practice on the entire alphabet until you can write all the letters in proper order from memory.

25. Words whose outlines are horizontal, as make (em-kay), or mimic (em-em-kay), should be written on the line.

26.   EXERCISE 2.

Take   make   hotel   jug   bank   oral

deluge   anthem   demolish   behead   Chicago   Louisiana.

Arm, mail, neck, early, fail, daily, bill, being, bell, lay, may, no, show, own, say, so, way, became, came, deluge, demolish, avenge, mimic, money, name, thick, wake, picnic, polish, shame, among, ask, death. Ascending letters, when initial, should begin on the line: Lady, love, head, heavy, lake, alarm, also, length, long, live. (2 min).

LESSON III.

WORD-SIGNS.

Lay   el   ish   shay   hay (not thus)   Alabama   behead   duet   keg   annul   period

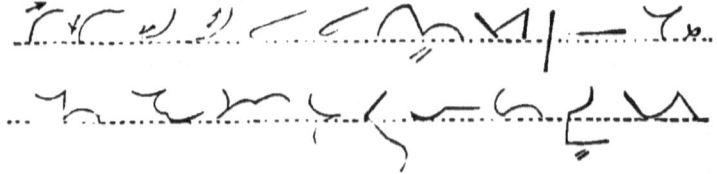

anatomy   nothing   asylum   fail   gypsy   ink   thumb   Asiatic   bishop

27. Proper names are underscored with a double dash, as in *Alabama*.

28. The initial tick of hay should be written in a horizontal position, and not allowed to incline in such a manner as to form a hook. It is sometimes inconvenient to write this tick when hay is medial. In such cases it is indicated merely, by retracing the preceding letter, as in *behead.*

29. Such words as *duet* and *key* are written with a single stroke of the pen, and should taper or thicken gradually.

30. The liquid *l* is sometimes written downward, and is then called *el* to distinguish it from *lay* (upward). Ish, when struck upward, is called *shay*. The student should always use lay and ish, unless el or shay is specified.

31. One of the purposes in sometimes using el instead of lay, and shay instead of ish, is to secure better angles at their junctures with other letters. The legibility of an outline depends to a large extent upon its angularity. For this reason, a distinct angle should be made in joining ith and ef, ef and en, ith and ing, as in *nothing,* and other letters making similar junctions.

32. The participial ending, *i-n-g,* is denoted by the consonant ⌣ing.

33. *Rem.* Legibility in short-hand is even more important than speed; for of what consequence is rapid writing, if the characters cannot afterwards be read? Legibility depends in part upon the accurate formation of the characters; but in order that a character may be formed accurately, it is not necessary to write it slowly; on the contrary, experienced stenographers produce the more perfect outlines with a somewhat rapid movement, just as an ornamental penman executes the most graceful curve or flourish with a quick stroke, rather than by tediously drawing it. The student should learn from the first to *write* the characters rather than *draw* them. It is a loss instead of gain to continue forming them slowly in order to secure mathematical precision.

34. The learner's method should be, to write a given word slowly several times, until its outline is well fixed in the mind; then write it rapidly, and continue doing so until it can be formed both accurately and quickly.

EXERCISE 3.

35. Wait, botany, bulk, behead, bar, damage, depth, deviate, dialogue, effect, efficacy, effigy, epitome, error, escape, wade, fare,

farm, obviate, remedy, policy, agency, apology, milk, army, eclectic, delay, am, waking, embody, engage, enough, envy, image, inch, indemnify, inform, ingenuity, intimacy, unto, invoke, involve, shape, know, month, nominate, nothing, comic, shadow, share, adore, allopathy, arc, assassin, asylum, azure, bachelor, baggage, bath, below, beneath, betime, both, buffalo, colleague, cab, cabbage, chaos, delay, demagogue, detach, detail, dialect, dig, dilemma, dish, dogma, effeminate, enigma, dull, epidemic, æsthetic, fair, far, fellow, fetch, fish, gash, gum, gush, gypsy, hack, hedge, hitch, honey, hook, hush, infect, ink, lavish, levity, link, lodge, log, monk, omit, pair, pang, pathetic, ramify, remove, shake, sham, shove, going, tank, thief, thumb, tick, timid, top, topic, vacate, fatigue, Anthony, Jacob, Lewis, Matthew, Timothy, Fanny, Lilly, Lucy, Dakota, Dick, Jack, Tennessee, Alabama, Louisiana, Asiatic. Using shay (upward), bishop; using el (downward), along, denial, vowel, manual, annul. (5 m.)

36. A large number of the commonest words are indicated by brief characters, called *Word-signs*. These are merely abbreviated forms expressing one or more of the principal sounds of the words they are used to represent,—as in long-hand are the abbreviations Rev., A. D., P. M., Co., Ans., etc. These are not arbitrary characters, but express some of the leading consonant or vowel sounds of the words for which they stand.

37. *Word-signs:* which, come, for, have, (they, them,) was,) shall,) usual-ly, will, him, your, together, think, object.

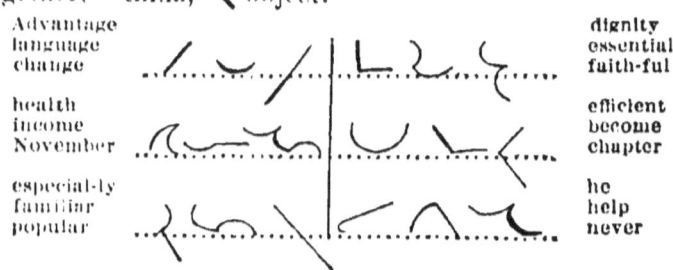

Advantage, language, change

health, income, November

especial-ly, familiar, popular

dignity, essential, faith-ful

efficient, become, chapter

he, help, never

38. The word-signs cannot be too thoroughly committed to memory, since the words they represent are those which recur the most frequently. Remember always to use the proper word-sign,

and not the full outline, whenever any sign-word occurs; e. g. use kay, never kay-em, for *come*; chay, not hay-way-chay, for *which*.

39. Write:

Will your big hack fetch my bulky baggage?

(6 times in 1 m.)

40. TRANSLATE.

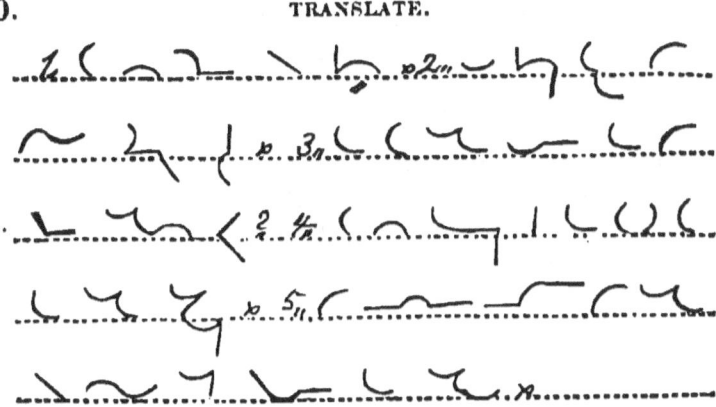

REMARK.—The engraving in this work is not perfect, particularly as to shading. A number of the light lines are too heavy. This, however, is not a serious fault; the same variance from an exact standard characterizes all actual reporting notes. The pupil may find the exercise a little more difficult to translate, but the training will be appreciated when, in after years, it becomes his duty to decipher characters which have been formed at verbatim speed.

SUGGESTION.—In learning lists a good plan is to write the words in a column at the left margin of a sheet of practice paper, afterwards filling each line by writing the word over and over rapidly. Always carry in your pocket some Short-hand book, manuscript or exercise to read at leisure moments, while traveling, waiting for cars or steamboats, for lazy people to keep appointments, or whenever an opportunity for a few minutes study may be had. The sign-book is suitable for this purpose.

LESSON IV.

RAY (or upward R), AND PHRASEOGRAPHY

41.

Are
wreck
ferry

forehead
tyranny
are-many

he-has-no
will-you-come
he-may-think

Rachel
heretic
allegory

he-hurried
he-may
he-was

he-is-wrong
are-you-ready

42. For the purpose of securing greater speed, angularity of outline, and also to prevent the too great downward tendency of many words, the liquid *R* is also written with an upward stroke, called *Ray*. This character is precisely like hay with the initial tick omitted.

43. The student should use ray in all cases where *ar* is not specified.

44. Using ray, write: Ring, road, revive, reveal, revenue, ready, repeal, rash, rate, range, wreck, wrong, abhor, apothecary, birth, bureau, arrive, earth, heretic, march, mark, marry, marriage, married, memorial (el), merry, admire, memory, mirror, narrow, notary, period, perish, rare, rarify, injury, theory, thorough, tornado, tyranny, variety, victory, hurry, ferry, poetry, Arizona, dare, allegory (el), arch, arduous, burial (el), bury, carry, cherry, cohere, forehead, forge, harsh, horror, inferior, morrow, ravage, red, repair, repel, retire, revenge, revoke, revolve, rich, rush, tardy, terror, torch, upright, urge, vary, verify, votary, wrath, wretch, notoriety, Darius, Ezra, Mark, Theodore, Marion, Mary, Rachel, Rosa, Ruth, Barrett.

45. *N. B.* Ray is more quickly written, and much oftener used than ar, and its employment more frequently secures angularity of outline.

46. Ar is always used before em, never before *te* or de, and rarely after kay; while ray is used after em, and before en and ing.

47. In lessening an outline, it is evident that either ar or ray makes a distinct angle by junction with a following kay or gay. The choice in such cases is determined in favor of ar by the fact of a preceding vowel, as in *arc*; but in the absence of such vowel, ray is used, as in *wreck*. Ray is employed, when final, if followed by a vowel, as in *ferry*.

48. WORD-SIGNS.

In, any		that
is, his		as, has
I		notwithstanding
you		are
rather		represent-ed
regular		irregular, argue
legible		illegible
reform		magazine
perform		magnanimous
New York		republic
majesty		peculiar-ity

PHRASEOGRAPHY.

49. In short-hand, two or more commonly recurring words are often written together, without the pen being lifted from the paper. An assemblage of words which may be thus joined, is called a *phraseogram,* and the character which expresses them, a *phraseograph.*

Much speed is gained by *phrasing,* with no sacrifice of legibility.

50. PHRASEOGRAPHS.

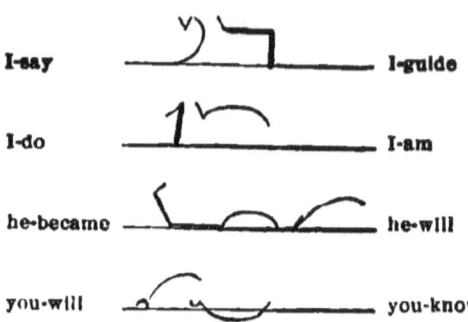

I-say — I-guide
I-do — I-am
he-became — he-will
you-will — you-know

51. In phraseography, only half the sign for I is commonly written, whichever "tick" makes the best angle with the word to which it is joined; *e. g.,* in *I-guide,* the downward stroke is used; but when the second tick is employed, it is *invariably struck upward,* as in *I-do.* With es, ze, ish, and zhe, the whole sign for I should be written, as in *I-say.*

52. The sign for *I,* when standing alone, or when it begins a phraseograph, is always written above the line, and the words combined with it must adapt themselves to its position. *E. g., I-am* is written above the line, although *am,* when it stands alone, is placed upon it.

53. *He,* in phraseography, is indicated by a tick precisely like the second stroke of the sign for *I,* excepting that it is *always struck downward,* as in *he-became.*

54. When this stroke does not make an angle with the following word, *he* may be expressed by the joined hay, written half its usual length, as in *he-hurried.*

55. *He,* different from *I,* has no position of its own, but adapts itself to that of the word to which it is joined. *E. g., he-may* is written on the line, while in *he-was* the tick is necessarily above the line.

56. The sign for *you* is inverted in phraseography, when necessary to secure a good angle, as in *you-know.*

PHRASEOGRAPHY.   27

57. *Are* is expressed by *ar* instead of *ray*, when angularity requires, as in *are-many*.

EXERCISE 4.

58. Join the words connected by a hyphen. I-think, you-are, I-am-going, he-will-be, he-has-no, you-will-have-them, he-may-arrive, I-abhor, I-perish, I-delay, you-represent, do-you-have, will-you-come.
1. He-may-think he-is-wrong. 2. Are-you-ready? 3. I-am-hurrying notwithstanding your delay. 4. I-am-going-into New-York. 5. He-will argue it. 6. I-shall reform-them. 7. I-think he-will-be popular enough as deputy. 8. I-say Tom will-do nothing for-them. 9. I-will-inform-you that-it-may-do for-March, never for-November. 10. His daily income will-make-him rich enough. 11. I-judge that Theodore will go-up into Dakota, Wyoming, especially Nevada. 12. Among-so-many, your book will-have-no advantage. 13. Ezra Barrett is rather peculiar. 14. They-may-never do-so. 15. Darius will-never-march any regular army into Arizona. 16. As-you-may know, his help, as-usual, is efficient. (4 m.)

59. Will-you-keep-your November-magazine for Mark Meredith? (4 times in 1 m.)

60.   TRANSLATE

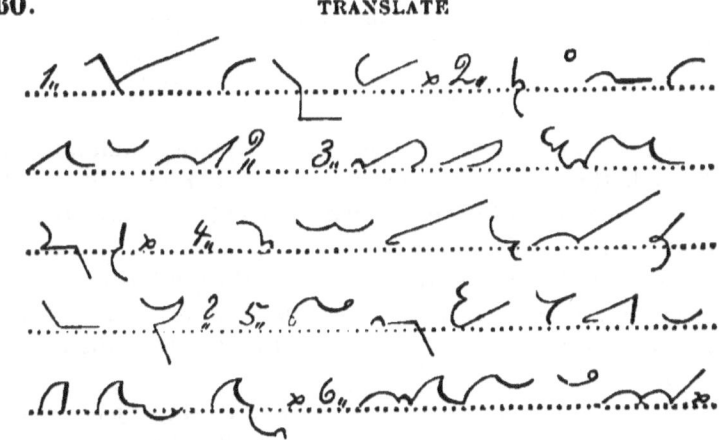

LESSON V.

LONG VOWELS.

61. SCALE.

e in *me*	aw in *law*
a " *make*	o " *ope*
a " *father*	oo " *boot*

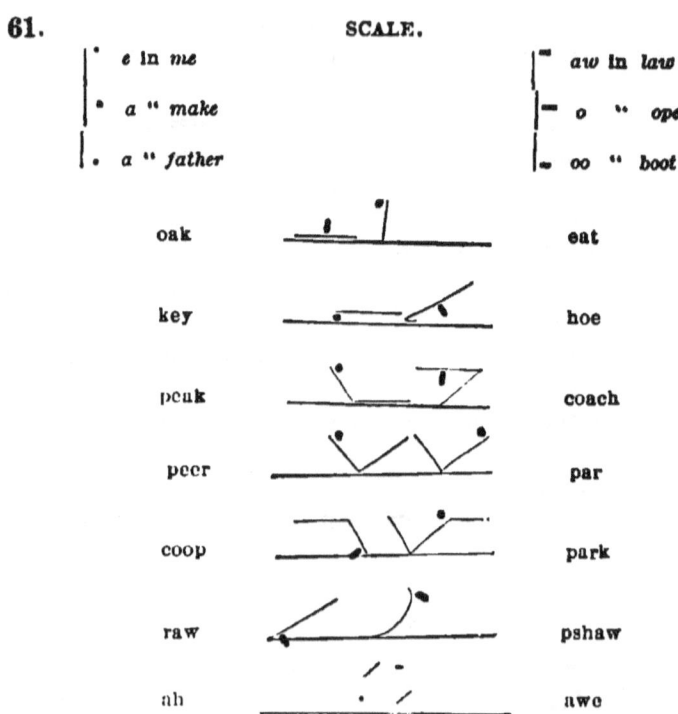

oak	eat
key	hoe
peak	coach
peer	par
coop	park
raw	pshaw
ah	awe

62. The six long vowels are denoted by a shaded dot and dash, placed beside the consonant signs at three different points, called the *first, second* and *third* vowel places, being respectively at the beginning, middle, and end of the consonant stem. The long sound of *e* is expressed by placing the large dot in the *first place*, or at the beginning of the consonant, as in *eat* or *key;* the sound of *o*, by writing the dash in the *second place*, or at the middle of the letter, as in *oak*.

63. These are denominated *first, second,* and *third place* vowels, according as they occupy the *first, second,* or *third* vowel positions.

64. Vowels placed above the horizontal, or at the left of the upright and slanting signs, are read before them, as in *oak* and *eat*. When placed below, or at the right of them, they are read afterward, as in *key* and *hoe*.

65. Dash vowels should invariably be written perpendicularly to the consonants beside which they are placed, as in *oak* and *raw*.

66. A word is said to be *vocalized* when the vowel signs are added to its outline. The *Nominal Consonant* is any letter, as te or chay, cancelled, its office being simply to indicate *position*, when words having no consonant are to be written, as *ah* and *awe*.

67. Vocalize: Eat, ate, tea, toe, ace, saw, sea, low, oaf, foe, oak, ache, key, coo, gay, aid, dough, awl, ale, lea, ape, Poe, paw, Joe, shoe, eve, thaw, pshaw, jaw, fee, aim, ma, woe, hoe, gnaw, knee, nay, Esau, row, raw, oar, era, ado, age, ah, aught, awe, bay, bee, fee, hay, Jew, low, oat, ode, sew, sue.

68. In the following words the vowel occurs between two consonants, and should be placed beside the first, as in *peak* and *coach*.

First place vowels: Beat, cheek, chalk, heap, heed, tall, leaf, league, leap, meal, peal, ball, beach, beak, beam, beer, hawk, kneel (el), leak, peach, peak, reap, sheep, team, teeth, wreath, wreathe, Neal (el), Paul, Maud.

69. *Second place:* Cake, coach, coal, comb, dale, dame, bail, bowl, cape, joke, fame, gale, game, jail, choke, knave, lame, loaf, nail (el), pole, porch, tale, tame, vale, yoke, abate, bore, roam (ar), rogue, rope, babe, bait, pale, dome, goal, loathe, mail, pail, poke, pope, rake, robe, tail, tape, vague, Job.

70. Third-place vowels should be written beside the second of the two consonants between which they occur, as in *coop:* Pool, tool, root, balm, boom, calm, rood, tomb; (using ar) lark, tar, czar, tour, jar.

71. Using only the long vowels: Antique, aurora (ar), bouquet, foliage, elate, jubilee, oatmeal, parade, pillow, pony, potato, uproar, yellow, Ada, Cora, Edith, Eva, Laura, Nora, lower (ar).

72. The lists of words given in this book as a rule should not be vocalized, except in special cases where one or two vowels are required to render an outline unambiguous. Isolated words commonly require vocalization.

73. *Rem.* Only one out of many hundred vowels is actually written in short-hand; but enough more are *indicated* by the manner of combining the consonant signs to make the system entirely legible.

The possibility of reading from the consonants alone may be shown by the fact that a page of print is easily decipherable, all the vowels having been previously blotted out; for not only would the spaces remain which set off the words, but those also which indicate where vowels are to be supplied. This crudely illustrates the method employed in short-hand.

74. A thorough acquaintance with the vowel signs is essential, nevertheless; that they may be written quickly in the few instances in which they are used, and that the principles of consonant combination by which they are indicated, may be understood. The long vowels, especially, should be well memorized, since they are employed much more frequently than the short.

75. The rule for placing vowels between two consecutive consonants must not be neglected; otherwise a vowel might be placed at the angle of two letters, which would occasion ambiguity; *e. g.*, pe-ray, with a large dot written within the angle, thus \./, may be read either *par* or *peer*.

76. CAUTION. The student must not forget that short-hand is written *by sound*. Vowels, in the sense here used, do not refer to the letters *a, e, i,* etc., but to the vocal sounds that are actually heard in the distinct utterance of any word. Hence, to write a word properly, no regard whatever should be had to its *spelling*. In *yoke*, for instance, there is but one vowel, that of *o long*; final *e*, being silent, is not represented. A good plan is to speak each word aloud before writing it; or, better still, to have the lists distinctly pronounced to you by another person.

77. The first vowel position being at the beginning of the consonant, first-place vowels should be written at the *top* of downward letters, as in *pshaw*, and at the *bottom* of the upward, as in *raw*.

78. As a rule, the vocalized words given in this and the two following lessons should always be written with the vowels.

79. To this, however, exceptions are sometimes made, especially in verbatim reporting, where time does not allow; also, in cases where any particular word occurs frequently in the same report, and for which the simple outline would be unmistakable.

LONG VOWELS.

80. WORD-SIGNS.

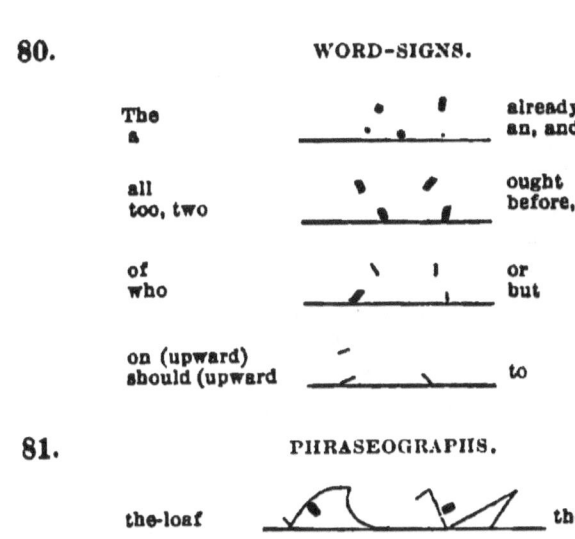

The, a		already, an, and
all, too, two		ought, before, oh
of, who		or, but
on (upward), should (upward)		to

81. PHRASEOGRAPHS.

the-loaf		the-porch
and-a		and-the
a-book-and		a-guide

82. Any one of the three ticks which denote *I* or *he* may be used to indicate *the*, that one always being selected which secures the best angle. This sign, when it represents *the*, invariably adapts itself to the position of the word to which it is joined; e. g., in *the-loaf*, it rests on the line, while in *the-porch*, it is one space above. No ambiguity can result from the use of the same sign for the article *the*, and the pronouns *I* and *he*.

83. *A, an, and*, are all denoted in phraseography by a brief tick, written horizontally or vertically (downward), as angle may require, as in *a-book-and a-guide*.

84. The dot, or vowel word-signs for *a, and, an*, and *the* are rarely used; only when the tick does not make a good angle.

EXERCISE 5.

85. The-day, the-object, the-usual, the-many, the-name, the-bishop, the-shadow, the-chapter, the-essential, and-it, and-do,

REPORTING STYLE OF SHORT-HAND.

and-go, and-make, and-will, and-know, and-represent, and-be, and-the, and-never, a-change, a-chapter, a-tornado, a-rather, an-illegible, and-you-may, and-he-may, and-I-may, and-I-will, a-lake-and-a-farm, a-long-delay, he-has-come-to take-the-magazine.

1. The-day is coming, and-you-may-look-for-a victory before-long. 2. Should-you-come-to-day, Maud and-Laura will-make-a bouquet and-an antique foliage wreath for-you. 3. Are-you-going-to-go-to sea to-day? 4. Paul, take-your oar and-go-and row a-league. 5. The-knave is-taking coal into-the coach. 6. They-have-a tall coop in-the park. (4 m.)

86. Cora, you-may-go-and help Laura make oatmeal cake for tea. (6 times in 2 m.)

87.   TRANSLATE.

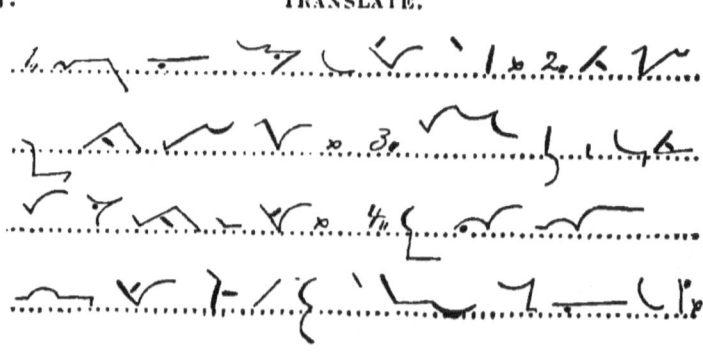

Note.—The vowels are used rarely; nevertheless they must be *thoroughly mastered*, in order that they may be inserted without a moment's hesitation when a rapid report is being made. The pupil is cautioned against forming the long-vowel signs too small, a common error, which results in confusing them with the short-vowels.

Suggestion.—It is well to encourage the tendency, which is quite natural, of picturing in one's mind the characters which represent words you hear spoken in conversation; also to cultivate the habit of mentally outlining and phrasing words and sentences. Word and phrase signs must be so thoroughly learned as to be written and read instantly. Spare hours may be given with advantage to writing and reading these abbreviations over and over many times.

LESSON VI.

DIPHTHONGS AND THE S-CIRCLE.

88.

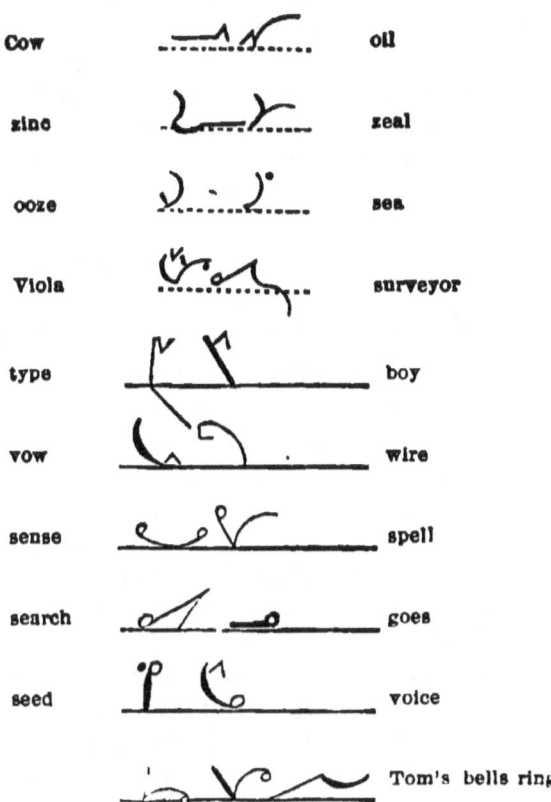

89. Write the following exercise, using the diphthongs *I*, as in *type*, *oi*, as in *boy*, *ow*, as in *cow*, and the triphthong *wi*, as in *wire*.

Tie, type, pipe, vile, knife, mile, defy, boy, boil, coil, oil, Illinois (el-en-oi), foil, row, vow, wire, toy, vouch, Guy, buy, chime, couch, cow, coy, dike, foul, hide, nigh, owl, fowl, pike, pile, rhyme, shy, sigh, spike, dye, thigh, tire, toil, annoy, diet, envoy, loyal, royal,

Isaac, sour (ar). Using long vowels also: assignee, voyage, Ely, Elijah, Eliza, Ida, Myra, Viola.

THE S-CIRCLE.

90. Es and ze are denoted in outlines by a small circle. This, when joined to *curved* letters, is written within, or following the direction of the curve, as in *sense*.

91. When joined to *straight* letters, the circle is always written upon the right of downward letters, as in *spell*; on the left of upward letters, as in *search*; and upper side of horizontal letters, as in *goes*. When the circle is initial, it is read before the vowels, as in *seed*, and when final, after them, as in *voice*.

92. TABLE OF S-CIRCLE JOININGS.

This table should be copied many times, until the student can without taking thought, join the circle properly. Written exercises should also be compared with it every day, until errors cease to be found. When joined to straight letters, the circle is executed from right to left, as the letter *o* is written in long-hand. This rule will enable the student to test the accuracy of his own work. For convenience in teaching, these characters are sometimes named, spe, pes, seb, bes, ste, tes, sed, des, sef, efs, sev, sith, sel, sem, ways, &c.

Es and ze, being cognates, are both represented by a single sign, namely, the circle, with no danger of ambiguity.

93. The circle is not employed, however, to denote ze, when initial, as in *zeal*, *zinc*, *zoology*, the full length consonant being used instead.

94. The possessive or plural of a word, which is formed in long-hand by the addition of *s* or *es*, is formed in short-hand by affixing the s-circle to its word-sign or outline; e. g., *Tom's bells ring*.

95. Es and ze, when standing alone, as in *ooze* or *sea*, cannot be represented by the circle, which it is impossible to vocalize.

96. Using the s-circle, write: Case, face, save, safe, sale, sake,

DIPHTHONGS AND THE S-CIRCLE. 85

said, same, eminence, endorse, famous, fix, harness, immense, less, Sabbath, safety, savage, scale, sell, senate, sense, sketch, small, smith, son, smoke, solid, slave, suppose, spell, study, sin, Sunday, space, this, yes, honesty, Saturday, alliance, announce, apologize, assets, audacious, avarice, cell, cemetery, debase, delicious, depose, devise, diffuse, dubious, factious, fictitious, notice, obvious, paradise, sex, sink, skip, sledge, slim, sling, slip, spare, spark, spool, such, sun, surface, surge, surpass, survey, surveyor, survive, swallow, swing, Swiss, switch, twice, valise, various, vase, vex, wages, wax, Horace, James, Marcus, Nicholas, Rufus, Samuel, Thomas, Stella; (using ar) cellar, circuitous, severe, Cæsar, enforce, force.

97. Vocalize: Lace, seal, seat, site, slow, snow, sail, choose, dose, abase, choice, geese, gaze, score, spoil, stay, vice, pause, voice, invoice, nice, noise, spy, ail, soul, chase, cheese, dice, entice, race, sage, sauce, siege, sky, slay, sleeve, slope, sly, snail, snake, soap, sole, spire, stale, sty, repose, sway, Maurice, Miles, Saul, Sarah; (using ar) soar, sore.

98.   WORD-SIGNS.

How, high, its, several, Savior, special, subject, advantageous.

EXERCISE 6.

99. 1. That boy of-yours makes enough noise. 2. Do-you-say he-is going-to tie the-rope to-the cow's neck? 3. He-ought-to-make less noise, so-that-he-may-keep his seat in-the-Senate. 4. May honesty be-your policy notwithstanding your name-may become less famous. 5. I-will-help-you take-an invoice of all-your-stock. 6. You-should-never for-any reason, or-on-any-day, make-a foolish vow. 7. Do-you indorse the-study of-such-a-subject as-this? 8. Yes, and-I-think-you-should study it thoroughly on-all-days but Sundays. 9. I-suppose you-will-make-it-your special object to know it all before-the-month of November. 10. Several boys have-come to-day to-sell milk. 11. You-will-have-no magazine for sale in-this-language for-several-days. 12.

It-was-said in-the-Senate of-Illinois that-for-the space-of two-days all bells should ring the-alarm. 13. The-Senate of-this-republic will-long-be famous for its safe and-dignified policy. (4m 30s).

100. How-many-days do-you-suppose he-will-be in-surveying enough-space for-the-cemetery? (10 times in 2 m).

101.   TRANSLATE.

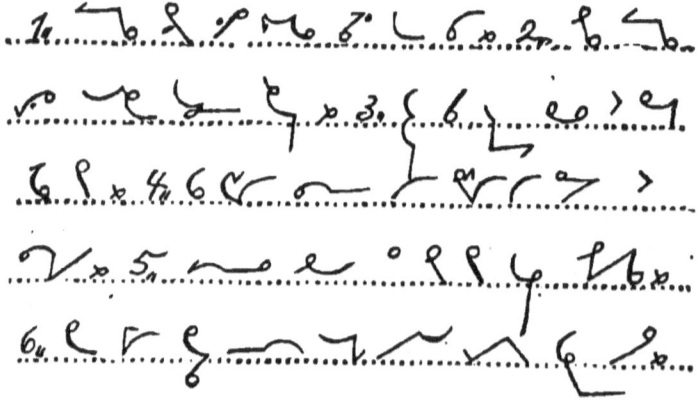

NOTE.—The pupil is cautioned against the error of forming the *s-circle* too large. There is little danger of getting it too small. Imitate the characters in the Table in section 92. The lines composing the diphthongal signs should invariably be made light, and the angle acute. It is the tendency of pupils to form these characters considerably larger than necessary.

SUGGESTION.—The student can in no case make real progress unless he accustoms himself to writing sentences he hears actually spoken. It is indispensable that the exercises be written as they are read aloud by some other person. As it is not always an easy matter to find a person sufficiently patient and reliable to serve the purpose, it is very desirable that two or more persons pursue the study together. Each then becomes interested in the other's progress, and the assistance and encouragement afforded by mutual study are well known.

LESSON VII.

SHORT VOWELS.

102.

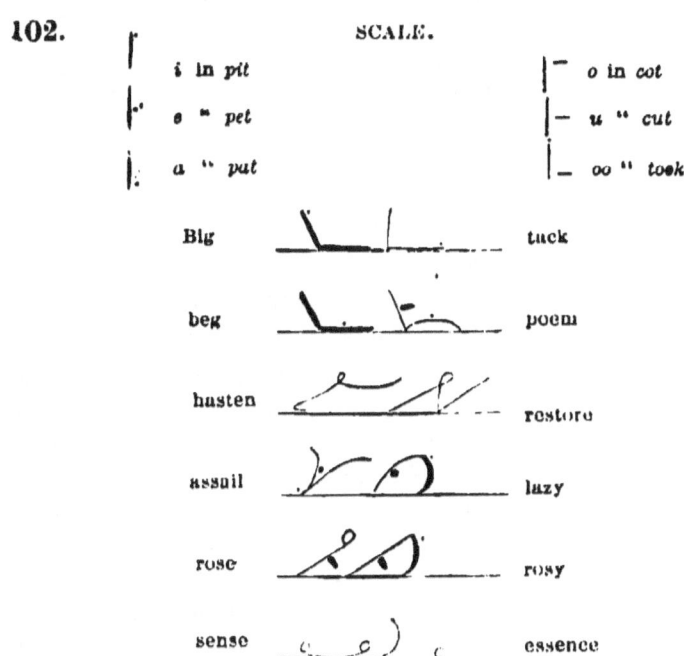

SCALE.

i in pit
e " pet
a " put

o in cot
u " cut
oo " took

Big — tuck
beg — poem
hasten — restore
assail — lazy
rose — rosy
sense — essence

The short-vowel signs differ from the long only in point of shade, the dot and dash being made large or small according as long or short vowels are to be expressed.

103. Write: Big, fill, ill, job, kick, kill, knock, lock, rock, chorus, echo, edge, egg, elbow, else, guess, kiss, mass, haughty, enemy, alas, Asia.

104. The following third-place vowels, coming between two consecutive consonants, should be placed beside the second, as in *tuck:* Tack, valley, malice.

105. Second-place short vowels, coming between two consecutive consonants, are placed beside the second, (unlike second-place long vowels, which are written with the first). Beg, cup, gem, autumn, lion.

106. When two vowels, either long or short, occur between two consecutive consonants, the first is placed beside the first consonant, and the other beside the second, as in *poem.* Idiom, idiot, poem, maniac.

107. The entire rule for placing vowels, both long and short, between two consecutive consonants is, briefly:

Write beside the first consonant;
> First-place long vowels,
> First-place short vowels,
> Second-place long vowels.

108. Beside the second consonant;
> Second-place short vowels,
> Third-place short vowels,
> Third-place long vowels.

 Diagram showing the assignment of vowels when occurring between two consecutive consonants.

109. Besides keeping vowels out of angles, a further advantage of this rule is that second-place vowels, though they be insufficiently or wrongly shaded, are known by the position which they occupy beside the first or second consonant.

No symbol is provided for the sound of *e* in *sermon*, which should be indicated by the sign for *e* in *met* (not by that for *u* in *up*).

Some other shades of vowel sound are not provided for in the short-hand vowel scale; but these, for all practical purposes, are clearly enough indicated by the signs for those vowels which most nearly approach them.

110. When two vowels are to be placed beside one consonant, they are written at unequal distances from it, according to the order in which the sounds occur, as in | − Dio.

INITIAL AND FINAL ES AND ZE.

111. Since the circle cannot be vocalized, when *es* follows an initial, or *es* or *ze* precede a final vowel, the stroke and not the circle *es* or *ze* is used; as in *assail* or *lazy.* This rule holds good in all cases, whether the vowels are actually written or not, since the use of the stroke consonant in these circumstances indicates where the vowels are to be supplied; e. g., the alphabetic letters are used in *essence* and *easy*, and the circle in *sense* and *rose*. Vocalize: Racy, mazy, dozy, posy, daisy, gauzy, dizzy, hazy, noisy, essence, espy.

112. In the following list, write both long and short vowels. Special attention should be paid to the proper placing of them beside the consonants.

Acme, agony, alimony, allure, ally, alto, apathy, apex, appal, appease, Arab, array, audit, bang, barrow, botch, buggy, cameo, chip, chop, cob, coffee, cog, dairy, duck, dumb, Dutch, epic, essay, ethics, flat, fogy, gang, gas, gaudy, hiatus, hobby, job, lag, lap, lash, latch, lath, leg, lip, luck, lung, mellow, melodious, mess, mob, odd, opera, palace, palm, parody, pith, rack, shock, silk, solemn, Stoic, tally, tear, Adam, Amos, Caleb, Ellis, Emory, Enoch, Jesse, Agnes, Alice, Anna, Ella, Emily, Emma, Hannah; (using ar) arrow, attire, err.

113. Without vowels: Veracious, custom, device, disengage, fallacious, auspicious, hasten, swell, visit, celerity, paradox, reason, receive, restore, race, raise, summer, service; (using ar) circus, erroneous, resume.

114.   WORD-SIGNS.

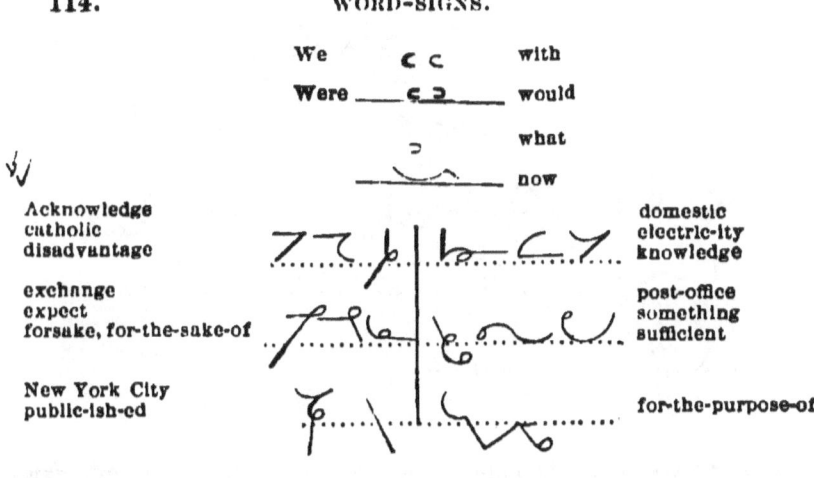

Acknowledge
catholic
disadvantage

exchange
expect
forsake, for-the-sake-of

New York City
public-ish-ed

domestic
electric-ity
knowledge

post-office
something
sufficient

for-the-purpose-of

EXERCISE 7.

115. 1. What-do-you guess is-in-the-post-office for-you?
2. I-think-it-is-a sketch, "The-Lion on-the Rock" being-the-sub-

ject, and-a poem on "The-Idiot and-the Maniac," wmch I-st.&
receive and-take-to-the notary. 3. Will-you-acknowledge that
the valley is hazy in autumn? 4. Yes, but it-is-never so in summer.
5. I-have-no-memory-of any-such tale as-that-in-your book.
6. To edit such-a-book is-a-big job. 7. It-is-in-no-way sufficient,
so-you-will-have-to exchange it for-something-else (el). 8. The-
enemy has knowledge-and-reason, but it-is erroneous to say-that-
he-has riches. 9. Shall we-take-the team and-buggy and-hasten
to-visit-the circus to-day? 10. It-is-the-custom with-them to eat
nothing but-milk-and-eggs on-Sunday. 11. All-the ships of-the
navy will soon sail into-the sea and-engage with-the haughty
enemy. (4 m.)

116. What-would-be-the-advantage in restoring the-domestic
customs of-a-race of-which-we-have scarcely any-knowledge?
(8 times in 2 m.)

117. TRANSLATE

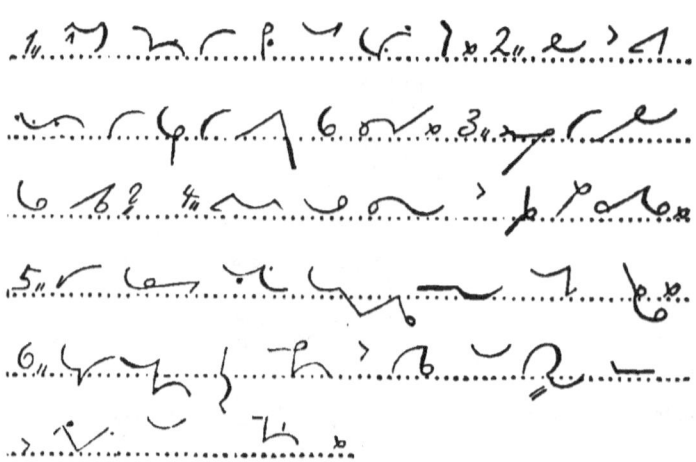

SUGGESTION.—When the pupil has arrived at this point the most advis-
able thing for him to do next is to turn back and learn lesson VII over
again. A knowledge of the vowels is much more important than the
space here given would seem to indicate.

LESSON VIII.

CONSONANT POSITION.

118.

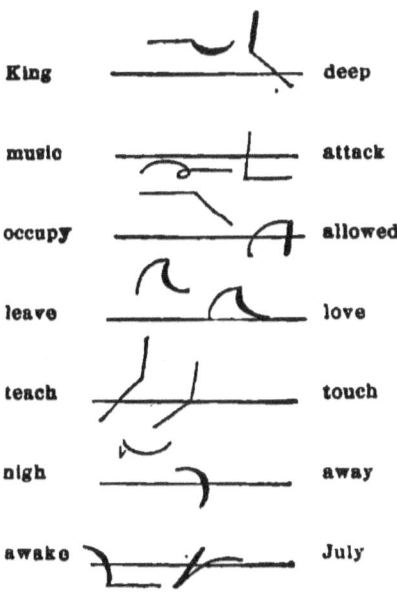

King — deep
music — attack
occupy — allowed
leave — love
teach — touch
nigh — away
awake — July

119. Among the contrivances made use of to indicate vowels without actually writing them, one of the most simple and important is that of *consonant position*. By means of this, the leading vowel of any word, that is, the vowel contained in the accented syllable, is denoted by the position given its outline.

120. With reference to the line of writing, words occupy three different places, known as the first, second, and third consonant positions.

121. *Second-position* words rest on the line, where all words heretofore introduced are written.

122. *First-position* horizontal words are written one space above the line, as *king*.

123. Other *first-position* words are written half a space above the line; e. g., in *deep*, *de*, the first descending letter, rests half a space above the line, *pe* being bisected by it.

124. *Third-position* horizontal words are written just below the line, as *music*.

125. Other *third-position* words rest half a space below the line; e. g., in *attack*, *te*, instead of resting on the line is bisected by it.

126. The *place* of the accented vowel is signified by the *position* of the outline. Writing a word in the first-position signifies that its accented vowel is first-place (as ee, aw, oi, etc.). E. g., short *o*, the accented vowel in *occupy*, is implied by the position of the word above the line. Writing it in the third position signifies that its accented vowel is third-place (ah, ow, oo, etc.). E. g., *ow*, the accented vowel in *allowed*, is signified by the position of the word through the line.

127. Write in *first-position:* Deal, abide, by, body, time, deep, deny, die, dime, she, ease, easy, easily, enjoy, fall, feel, female, joy, joyous (jay-es), king, law, leave, lie, life, life-time, like, me, meek, avoid, mill, my, occupy, thy, thee, if, off, pity, see, talk, teach, week, weak, assign, write, right, reach, alleviate, cheap, Deity, dock, dominate, miss, mock, nick, seam, series, size, speedy; (ar) fear, form, fire, sphere.

128. *Third-position:* Allow, assume, at, out, atom, attach, attack, beauty, back, cap, catch, cash, cavity, cool, aloud, allowed, few, hat, huge, Jewish, jury, lack, lad, laugh, map, match, mouth, move, path, view, abuse, academy, academic, eulogy (el-jay), fool, loose, factory, outrage, pure, renew, review, ruin, add, adduce, ensue, lose, pack, purity, purify, salute, sat, suit; (ar) power, poor, room, our, hour.

Exceptional words, 3rd. pos.: Away, awake, await, July, advice.

129. Evidently the greatest speed is attainable when one position only is observed in writing. For this reason, words are commonly placed on the line, and are put in other positions only when speed is actually gained by it, that is to say, when they would otherwise have to be vocalized, which would require more time than the other. It must not be supposed that all words which contain first or third place accented vowels, are to be written in the first or third positions. These are made use of only when the writing of vowels can thereby be saved. It is a frequent case of two or more words having the same consonant outline, none of which need vocalizing, if all are different parts of speech. But ambiguity would result from the use of lay-ve to represent the two verbs *love* and *leave*. In this case, the writing of vowels, otherwise necessary, is saved by placing *leave*, which contains the first-place vowel, in the first position. The use of te-chay for both *touch* and *teach* would also be ambiguous; hence, to denote *teach*, this outline is also written in the first position.

130. But it sometimes transpires that the accented vowels of both words are second place, as in the case of *wait* and *await*. This would determine both for the second position; but nevertheless, as a matter of convenience in such cases, one of the words is written in either the first or third position, according as some unaccented first or third place vowel which it may contain, would indicate. E. g., *await* and *awake* are written in the third position, in order to be distinguished from the second position words, *wait* and *wake*, which have the same outlines.

131. In all such cases the most commonly recurring word is given the second position.

132. Vocalized words commonly occupy the second position; but the legibility of short-hand writing is increased by occasionally giving these also the positions indicated by their accented vowels. This is more especially practiced in the case of words with horizontal outlines, as *nigh*, *sky*, etc.

133. WORD–SIGNS—1ST POS.

Common, each, watch, ear, hear, her, ever, give-n, dollar, thing.

EXERCISE 8.

134. 1. You-may-write-a review of all-our doings at-the-academy on-the fourth Sunday of-February. 2. We-all know-that fire ruins many factories and-mills. 3. You-may-copy off-the eulogy on-the-life, laws, and-power of-the Jewish king. 4. Talks on-the-subject of-electricity will-be given-in-both academies in-the-month of July. 5. It-is-a-common-thing-to hear her laugh aloud at-that huge fool's-cap. 6. I-will carry that small watch this-week, and-if-the-right time it-keeps, I-will-give-you $25.00 for-the-same. 7. The-judge said-that the-jury should occupy this cool room, and-at no-time be allowed to-leave-it before -they say what-the damages in-this-case shall-be. 8. It-is-our-custom to-sell-for cash, but-you-will-be allowed to-exchange your-map for-a hat or cap, or anything-else (el) that-you-may lack. 9. The-huge earth moves along-its path many-miles an-hour. (4m).

135. To-study the-lives-and laws of-the Jewish kings is-a-common-thing in-our day-and-age. (9 times in 2m).

136.   TRANSLATE.

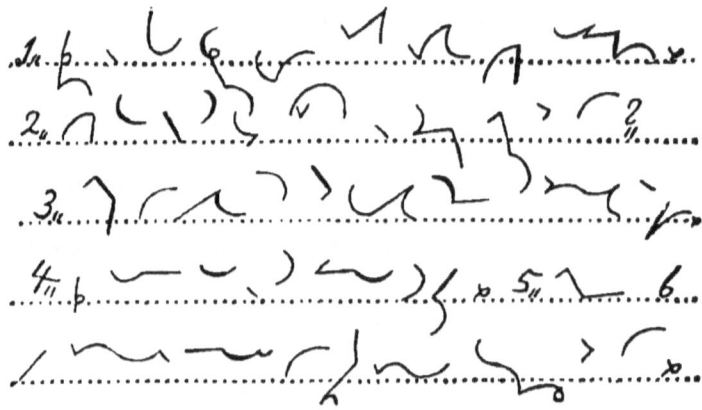

REMARK.—It is a common misapprehension that every word whose accented vowel is first or third place, ought on this account to be written in the first or third position. The great mass of words are written in the second position, that is, on the line. The writing of words elsewhere than on the line is a contrivance, the principal use of which is to save writing the vowels in the case of a limited number of frequently recurring words, whose outlines would be ambiguous if written in the second position, and left unvocalized. If necessary to prevent ambiguity it is better to vocalize an uncommon word rather than to attempt to indicate the vowels by placing its outline in the first or third position.

LESSON IX.

137.   **S-CIRCLE JUNCTIONS.**

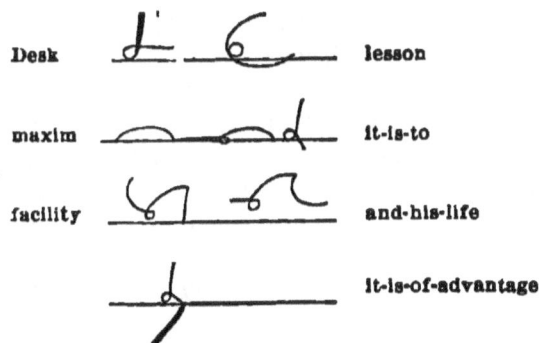

138. The rule laid down in Lesson VI. for joining the s-circle, applies only when it occurs at the beginning or end of words.

139. But when the circle occurs at the juncture of two consonants, it should be written according to the following directions:

140. When the circle is to be written—

1. At the juncture of two straight letters, it should be placed outside the angle, as in *desk*.

141. 2. At the juncture of a straight letter and a curve, it should follow the direction of the curve, as in *maxim*.

142. 3. At the juncture of two curves, if it cannot follow the direction of both, as it does in *lesson*, it should be written in the manner found most convenient, as in *facility*.

143. These directions apply also to phraseographs; e. g., *it-is-to, and-his-life, it-is-of-advantage*.

144. In the following list, the s-circle occurs between two straight letters: Custody, deposit, desk, dispatch, discuss, disobey, dispose, exhibit, dispel, expel, gazette, gospel, indispose, justice, succeed, capacity, Mexico, Tuesday, audacity, besiege, bestow, caustic, chastise, luxury, depository, disguise, despair, dusk, exodus, expire, extinguish, gasp, gossip, hostile, outside, parasite, receipt, restless, upset, *et-cetera*, Augustus, Justus, Augusta.

145. Between a straight and curved letter: Citizen, desire, desirous, disarm, dislike, dismal, dismay, dissolve, egotism, excel, Harrison, immensity, maxim, maximum, message, music, resolve, cohesive, instil, musical, pacific, society, solicit, specify, vestige, veracity, Massachusetts, Minnesota, axiom, answer, castle, casualty, decimal, dismiss, dissolve, elastic, exile, felicity, garrison, offset, pacify, parasol, spasm, specify, tenacity, velocity, visitor, Absalom, Erastus (ar), Joseph, Missouri.

146. Between two curves: Atheism, counsel (el), facility, incendiary, innocence, insanity, lesson (el), mason, muscle, pencil (el), vessel (el), Cincinnati, officer, despair, exterior, risk, rustic, cancel (el), sarcasm (ar), chancellor (el), counsellor (el), damsel, denizen, domicile, fasten, gymnasium, license, lyceum, offensive, submissive; (also) salary, search, decorus, solitary, sophomore, sorrow, story, sir (ar), scarce (ar), genius, malicious, science, select, sublime, Minneapolis.

147. WORD-SIGNS—3 POS.

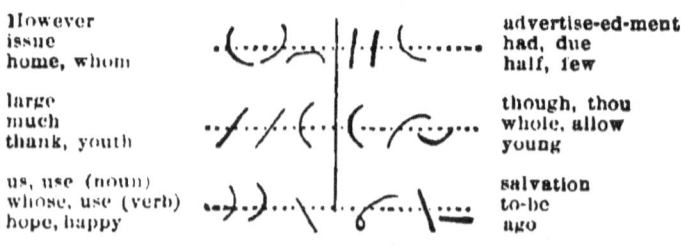

However	advertise-ed-ment
issue	had, due
home, whom	half, few
large	though, thou
much	whole, allow
thank, youth	young
us, use (noun)	salvation
whose, use (verb)	to-be
hope, happy	ago

EXERCISE 9.

148. 1. The-Gazette says that Harrison's army will-leave Mexico on-Saturday of-this-week, and-march all-the-way-to Minneapolis, Minnesota, by-way-of-Missouri. 2. The-citizen deposits his salary in-the-bank-of Massachusetts with-scarcely any risk. 3. The-rustic, taking-counsel with-the judge for half-an-hour, says nothing, but for-some purpose dispatches his son to-Cincinnati. 4. The-justice informs counsel that-they-may, if-they wish, discuss-the-case before-the-jury for-two-hours. 5. Do-you-think-that-the jury will-say the-youth is insane? 6. Yes, they-have already said-so; he-receives-the-message in despair, and-many also receive-it with sorrow and-dismay. 7. The-officers are-taking him into-custody, and-will keep-him safely in-a solitary room. 8. The-young sophomore, they-say, has-a rare genius for poetry and-music. 9. I-hope the-saying has-no sarcasm in-it. 10. I-know, however, that-he-excels in-science, and-never fails to exhibit vivacity in-society. 11. Instil right maxims into-the soul of-a-youth, and-you-will see that-his life will-be-the purer. (4m. 80 s.)

149. I-hope, however, that-you-will give-the-youth whom-you teach the-whole story of young Absalom. (8 times in 2 m.)

150. TRANSLATE.

DICTATION PRACTICE.—When two or more persons meet together for dictation practice the following plan may be adopted: Be seated all at one table. Limit your attention to the lesson upon which you may be engaged. Do not practice for speed upon any exercise until you have first learned to phrase and outline it correctly. Each student should in turn read to the other members of the group. Write the list-words a number of times, reading them as often. Dictate slowly at first, gradually increasing the speed. Afterwards determine which student is able to read the entire list in the shortest time. In dictating an exercise, read the sentences in the natural way, as they would be delivered by a public speaker, allowing the intervals to occur between clauses rather than between words.

LESSON X.

151.   **PHRASEOGRAPHY.**

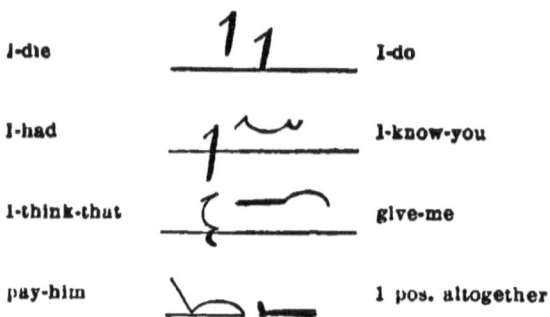

152. Every stenographer must determine for himself the precise extent to which he can apply *phraseography* to advantage. Many do not phrase enough; while, possibly, some do too much. Students, accustomed in long-hand to disjoin words, invariably find phraseography a hindrance at first; but the practice, once acquired, lessens the labor of reporting, and adds to both speed and legibility. Three words can be phrased while two of them are being written separately; hence the gain in speed. But *words separated by the slightest rhetorical pause, or mark of punctuation, should not be joined together.* This adaptation of phraseography to syntax, renders short-hand notes far more legible than they would otherwise be.

153. The first word, which is called the *Leader*, should be written in its proper position, and the others allowed to occupy whatever place the paraseograph, in due course, may give them. E. g., *I* is the leader of the phrase, *I-think-that; give*, the leader in *give-me*, etc.

154. But many phraseographs can be so written that both the leader and word to which it is joined, shall occupy their appropriate positions, as in *I-had*.

155. The necessity phraseography imposes upon the writer of locating words out of their proper positions, occasions no drawback upon legibility. The reader does not regard the position of

PHRASEOGRAPHY.

words after the first or second, but relies upon the context, which is a sure guide.

156. The phraseograph should be discontinued when an unusual word occurs, or one which must be written in its proper position in order to be unambiguous. E. g., *give him*, and *pay me*, should not be joined, for fear of conflict with *give-me*, and *pay-him*.

157. 1 pos. (using the s-circle): Cause, cease, city, office, oppose, peace, rise, seen, scene, sing, accede, seem, seed, seek, side, sight, since, police, these, wise, song, besides, disease, deceit, deceive, decide, design, despise, decease, excite, exceed, false, insight, incite, inside, likewise, business, mix, offence, scheme, Scotch, sleep, sweep, epistle, alike (el), misery, reside, resign, revise, righteous, sincere, recite, rejoice, arise (ar).

158. 3 pos.: Amuse, soon, accuse, pass, passage, passive, sad, sagacity, anxiety, nuisance, induce, excuse, anxious, animosity, atlas, casual, beauteous (be-tes), absence, apostle, south, subdue, task, tax, absorb, refuse, house, refusal, rescue, reduce.

Also write (3 pos.), anatomy, animate; (ar), affair, argue.

159.   WORD-SIGNS.

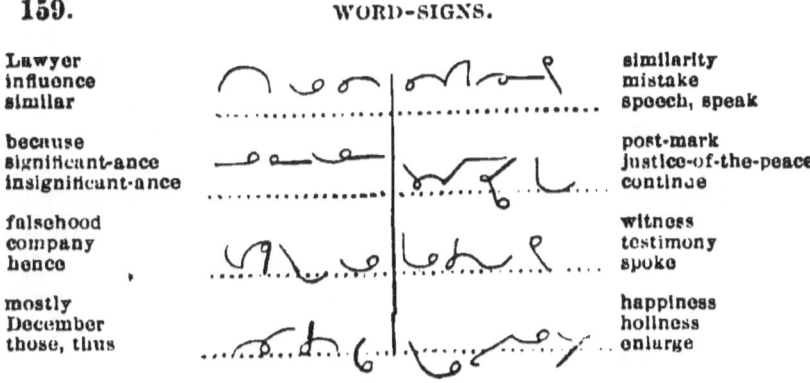

Lawyer		similarity
influence		mistake
similar		speech, speak
because		post-mark
significant-ance		justice-of-the-peace
insignificant-ance		continue
falsehood		witness
company		testimony
hence		spoke
mostly		happiness
December		holiness
those, thus		enlarge

EXERCISE 10.

160. 1. A-rogue, whose name is Esau, takes-away the-cow of Paul the-rustic. 2. He-also carries off some of Paul's sheep, and-designs taking-his dog too. 3. But-the dog barks, and-Esau fearing he-will-be-seen, hastens home. 4. Paul informs-an-officer, who, with-the-help of-the-police, soon-succeeds in arresting-the rogue. 5. They-take-the anxious Esau to-the city, and-lock him in-the-south room of-the jail. 6. Esau is accused by Paul of-having carried off-his live-stock. 7. Esau denies all knowledge of-the affair, and-goes to seek-the advice of counsel. 8. He-goes-to-the office of-the sagacious Scotch lawyer, Jackson, who, sitting pensive in-his chair, asks-him what he-wishes. 9. I-have come, says Esau, to induce you to-argue in-my behalf in-the-cause in-which I-am-accused by Paul. 10. But-the lawyer, refusing to-help-him, says, I-think-you-will-never pay me. 11. At-the sight, however, of-the rogue's pile of-money, Jackson informs-him that-his side of-the-case is-the-right-side. 12. Esau, rejoicing exceedingly, says he-hopes it-is-no-mistake. 13. The-cause comes on for hearing before-a-jury and-a justice-of-the-peace, whose-name is Isaac. 14. The-lawyer Jackson thinks because both-the Justice and-the-accused are Jews, that-it-would-be-a wise scheme to-have-the Squire dismiss-the-jury, and-with-no-help to hear and-decide the-cause. 15. Hence the-accused, by-his-lawyer, moves-the Squire that-this-be-carried out; and-the-Justice so deciding, the-jury goes. 16. The-Justice sits and-hears the-testimony of-each witness in-the-case, which-is altogether insufficient to show that-the-accused is-the thief. 17. The-lawyer thinks-it useless to-make-a speech, and-so leaves-the-case wholly at-the disposal of-the-Squire. 18. The-Justice says the-accused may rise up, and-Esau does-so with-no-fear. 19. The-Justice also says: "The-bulk of-the testimony is insufficient to show-you to-be-the th ef; but I-rather think-that-the testimony is mostly wrong. 20. Hence, what-I-decide in-this-case is-this; that-you continue in-jail for-two-weeks, and-also that-you pass two-weeks on-the public rock-pile!" (8 m. 30 s.)

161. As-to-his design in-seeking-the house of-the justice-of-the-peace, the-witness spoke-a-falsehood in-giving-his testimony to-the-jury. (7 times in 2 m.)

NOTE.—When practicing write the characters as closely together as convenient, forming them somewhat smaller than is natural for you. This practice contributes both to speed and ease.

162. TRANSLATE

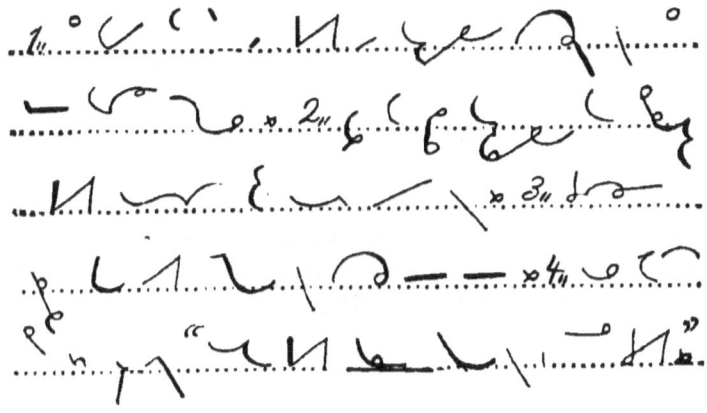

LESSON XI.

THE SEZ-CIRCLE, EMP, AND COALESCENTS.

163.

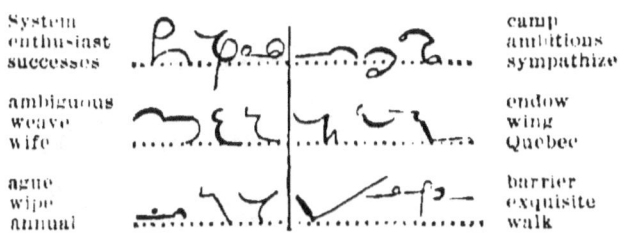

System		camp
enthusiast		ambitions
successes		sympathize
ambiguous		endow
weave		wing
wife		Quebec
ague		barrier
wipe		exquisite
annual		walk

164. The syllables sis, sys, sez, ces, sus, and others similar, are denoted by a large circle, as in *system* and *successes*.

Write: Cases, paces, necessary, success, successor, subsist, decisive, desist, excess, excessive, exercise, exist, hypothesis, necessity, insist, system, emphasis, emphasize, analysis (el). Mississippi, Texas, Jesus, exercises, successes, accessory, axis, diagnosis, enthusiast, recess, suspicious, thesis, possessor, Moses; 1 pos., exhaust.

⌒ EMP.

165. The cognates pe and be, when occurring after em, are sometimes indicated by a shading of this consonant, as in *camp*, or *ambitious*. This thickened em is called *emp*, and has the force of em-pe, or em-be.

166. Write: Pump, ample, camp, campaign, damp, encamp, example, lamp, lump, sample, sympathy, sympathize, temple, ambitious, imbecile, ambassador, ambiguity, ambiguous, embark, embellish, embezzle, empire, limp, pomp, symbol, symptom, thump.

TABLE OF COALESCENTS.

167. The signs here given have the force of the full-faced type in the corresponding words.

		LONG.			SHORT.	
W SERIES.	We		walk	with		wot
	wave		woke	wet		worst
	was		woo	twang		wool
Y SERIES.	ye		yawn	yi		yon
	yea		yoke	yet		young
	yarn		you	yam		.
TRIPHTHONGS.	wife		wound			

MNEMONIC FIGURES.

W dash coalescents bow to right.   Y dash coalescents bow upward.
" dot   "   "   " left.   " dot   "   "   " downward.

COALESCENTS.

168. The unobstructed consonants *w* and *y* are commonly called coalescents, from the quality which they possess of readily uniting, or *coalescing*, with the vowel sounds. The double sounds *we, ye, you*, etc., formed by combining *w* or *y* with a succeeding vowel, are frequently expressed by a small semi-circle written in the three vowel places, as *wa* in *wave*, *ya* in *yarn*.

169. Write: Dwell, wade, duke, hew, mule, muse, quack, squeeze, wed, wet, wood, Hugh, Julius, Luke, Celia, Delia, Eugenia, Utah.

170. When convenient, first and third place coalescents and diphthongs are joined to the consonant stems in connection with which they occur, as in *weare, wife, endow, highly*.

171. Write: Walk, wash, equip, ice, endow, Irish (shay), irony (ar), item, liquid, war, weave, wife, wit, wing, Idaho, Quebec, ague, dew, nephew, weed, widow, wipe.

Omitting the coalescents: Acquiesce, anguish, annual (el), avenue, barrier, exquisite, genial (el), ingenious, languish, luxurious, requisite, tedious; 3 pos., cube, cubic, duel.

PHRASEOGRAPHY.

172. The principles of abbreviation explained in this lesson are also made use of in phraseography. In ⌒ *may-be*, for example, ⌒, the sign for *may*, is shaded to denote the following ╲ *be*. ⌒ Emp in this case is in reality an abbreviated phraseograph, and is called a *phrase-sign*. The words "is-said" are expressed by the phrase-sign *sezde*, which is obtained by enlarging the circle in *said*. A phrase-sign is a contracted outline representing a number of words as though they were but so many syllables; whereas a phraseograph is obtained by merely linking a number of words together.

173. The coalescent and diphthongal signs are always written in a vertical or horizontal position, and do not, like the dash vowels, adapt themselves to their consonant stems by always being written at right angles with them.

174. The sez-circle should be written several times larger than the simple s-circle, so as to be readily distinguishable from it.

175. WORD AND PHRASE SIGNS.

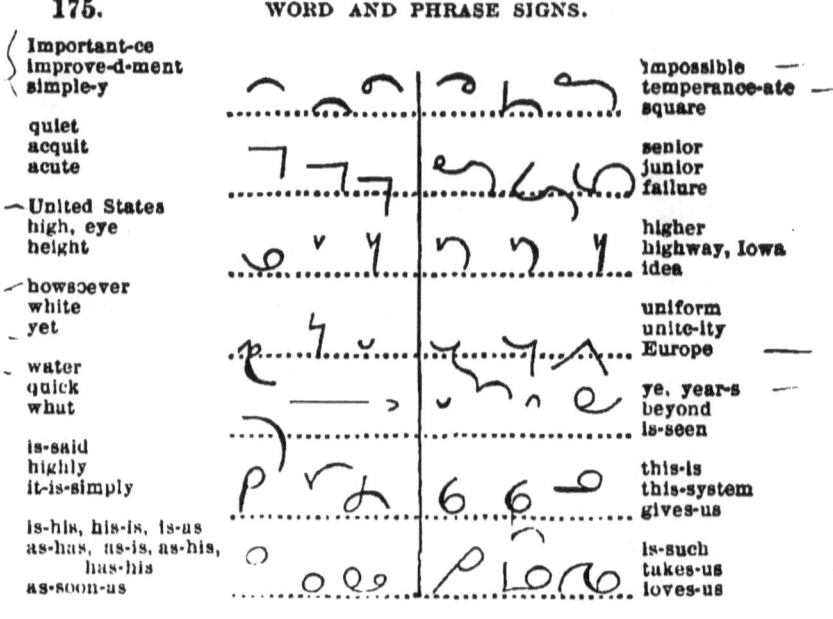

Important-ce
improve-d-ment
simple-y

quiet
acquit
acute

United States
high, eye
height

howsoever
white
yet

water
quick
what

is-said
highly
it-is-simply

is-his, his-is, is-us
as-has, us-is, as-his,
    has-his
as-soon-us

impossible
temperance-ate
square

senior
junior
failure

higher
highway, Iowa
idea

uniform
unite-ity
Europe

ye, year-s
beyond
is-seen

this-is
this-system
gives-us

is-such
takes-us
loves-us

EXERCISE 11.

176. 1. You-may-write-this and-all-succeeding exercises with red ink, if-you-wish, but-we-would-rather you-would-use simply the-common ink. 2. The-Yankee's Irish wife said she saw-a-large lamp sitting on-the top of the white temple. 3. Our temperance-speaker possesses a-genius for war, and-is-quick in-wit, with-which he-unites much irony. 4. He-has-an idea of uniting Texas, Iowa, Idaho, and-Utah by-a-common highway, but-the-thing is-simply-impossible. 5. This-is-our regular summer uniform, and-is-seen-in-the United-States-camps always at-this-time of year, but-is-never-to-be seen-in Europe. 6. He-loves-us, and-it-may-be that-that is why he-would-have us enjoy so-many of-the exquisite views in Utah. 7. Hugh takes-us to see-many sample dwellings on-the avenue, but I-think-that-many-of-them lack-some necessary improvements. 8. How-many-years will-it-be, do-you-think, before-this-system will-have come-into common use in-the United States, especially in-the large cities? 9. Our sagacious justice-of-the-peace subsists by hearing and-deciding various petty cases. (5 m).

DOUBLE CONSONANTS. 55

177. That-the-health of-the United-States army may-be-improved, it-is-important-that all-officers should set-an example of-temperance to inferiors. (11 times in 3 m).

178.   TRANSLATE.

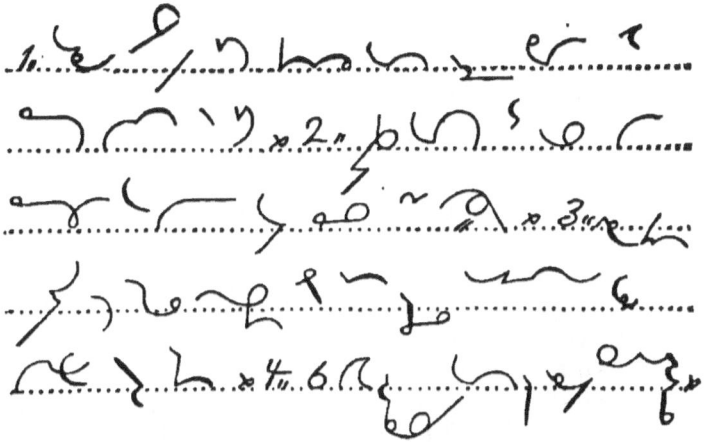

☞ See page 184 for the sign for "nevertheless."

LESSON XII.

DOUBLE CONSONANTS.—THE L-HOOK.

179. The liquids *l* and *r*, by reason of the vowel element which they possess, partially coalesce with other consonants which immediately precede them: *e. g.*, *l* unites very nearly with *p* in *play*, and with *f* in *fly*; *r* unites closely with *p* in *pry*, and with *f* in *offer*. These consonant double-sounds are of very frequent occurrence in our language, and are usually expressed by a modification of the stem of the first consonant.

THE L-HOOK.

180. The consonants of the l-hook series are:

Pel bel tel del chel jel kel gel fel vel thl thel shel (upward).

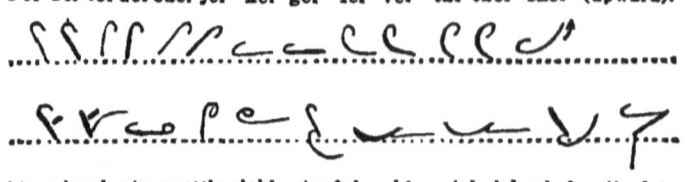

blow bowl glass settle sickle playful ankle nickel bushel collegiate

181. To express the added *l*, straight consonant letters are written with a small hook at the beginning, placed on the right, or s-circle side; *e. g.*, this character ⸜, called pel, has the force of pe-lay, as in *playful*. This hook is written within, or following the direction of curved letters.

182. These hooked, or double letters, are vocalized like other consonant stems, as in *blow*, or *glass*. But the double letter is not used if the vowel occurs between the two consonant sounds denoted by it; *e. g.*, in *bowl*, the hook cannot be employed, the vowel *o* coming between be and lay; but in *blow*, the double consonant bel is used, no vowel occurring between be and the liquid, *o*, the only vowel in the word, being final.

183. The s-circle is prefixed to double consonants of the l-hook series by being written within the hook, as in *settle* and *sickle*.

184. The adjective ending *ful* is usually expressed by the double consonant *fel*, as in *playful*.

185. All hooked consonants should be written with *one stroke of the pen*. This practice not only increases the speed of writing, but lessens the liability to form the hook too large or too cramped.

186. Write: Ankle, angle, assemble, assembly, available, battle, black, blame, blameless, blank, blush, chapel, circle, claim, class, clergy, climax, close, club, clumsy, clothe, declaim, diploma, double, emblem, employ, enclose, English, entitle, fable, faculty, festival, imply, implicit, globe, legal, illegal (el), inflame, level, local, mingle, admirable, novelty, noble, oblige, obstacle, parable, place, pledge, poetical, radical, reflect, stable, staple, table, technical, tremble, total, dimple, unable, social, syllable, delicacy,

THE L-HOOK.

uncle, variable, vital, vocal, ability, Florida, display, disclaim, disclose, exclaim, invisible, possible, visible, academical, acclimatize, amiable, amicable, bashful, Bible, blemish, bliss, block, blossom, cattle, chemical, classify, closet, coeval, collegiate, couple, culpable, declivity, despicable, devil, displace, dissemble, Episcopal, fallible, fatal, flesh, fling, flour, fluency, foretell (ar), gable, glimpse, gloom, horrible, invariable, inviolable, jingle, joyful, label, miserable, naval, nimble, pistol, placid, plague, plank, plastic, plausible, pliable, pliant, plum, plump, plus, ply, rival, shelf, shingle, smuggle, stubble, subtile, survival, tackle, tangle, terrible, tickle, tumble, typical, village, vehicle, wrinkle, Clarence, Hannibal, Clara, Flora, Florence; (using ar) clear, clerk, declare, implore, deplore, desirable, ramble, irresistible (sez); (vocalize) applause, bleak, clay, clue, fleece, glue, plume, ply, Abel, Michael, Mabel, blue; 1 pos. audible, awful, clock, clog, gloss, clause, climb, calling, evil, feeble, initial, liable, likely, official, please, reply, title, idle; 3 pos. allowable, anatomical, clash, clasp, pupil, suitable, affable.

187. WORD AND PHRASE SIGNS.

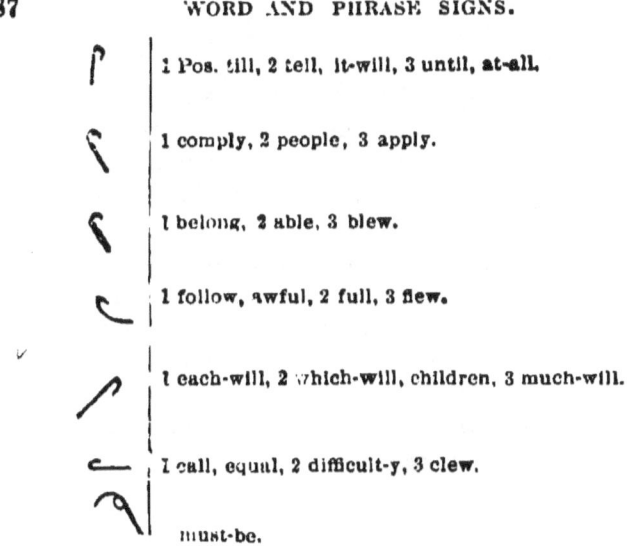

1 Pos. till, 2 tell, it-will, 3 until, at-all.

1 comply, 2 people, 3 apply.

1 belong, 2 able, 3 blew.

1 follow, awful, 2 full, 3 flew.

1 each-will, 2 which-will, children, 3 much-will.

1 call, equal, 2 difficult-y, 3 clew.

must-be.

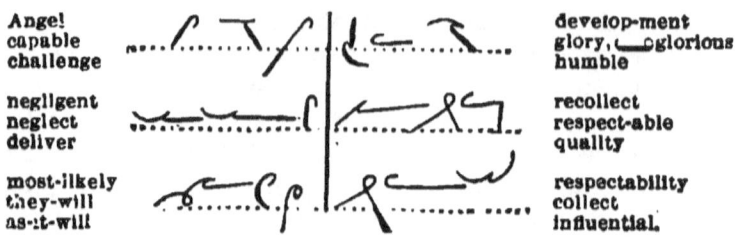

Angel capable challenge		development glory, glorious humble
negligent neglect deliver		recollect respect-able quality
most-likely they-will as-it-will		respectability collect influential.

188   EXERCISE 12.

1. Philosophy will clip-an angel's wings. 2. It-will never-do at-all for-you to-emphasize the-wrong syllable in-class. 3. Official people say they-will in-time become-respectable and-influential, which-will-be a-glorious-thing, if each-will at-the same-time be humble. 4. You-should use this-system as-soon-as you-are-able; much-will-be-the-time-that it-will-save-you, because-it-is-as speedy as-any, besides being-far easier. (1m 45s).

189.   THE-ASP AND-THE EAGLE.—ÆSOP.

1. This-fable tells of-a snake declaring war on-an-eagle, and-how they-engage in-fearful battle. 2. They-display no delicacy, nevertheless they-never-make-the air vocal with-the-clash of-arms or-the thump of-clumsy clubs. 3. The-snake has-the-advantage, and-will-likely kill-the-poor eagle. 4. But-a rustic sees them, and-hurrying, he-comes-up and-looses the-coil of-the-snake, and-allows the-eagle to fly away. 5. The-escape of-the eagle inflames the-snake, so-that-he allows his poison to fly into-the water bottle of-the rustic. 6. The-rustic, knowing-nothing of-the-possible evil, applies the-bottle to-his lips. 7. But-the eagle, flying back, delivers him, by-giving his right-arm a-blow with-his wing, and-by seizing the-bottle with-his claws, and-carrying it-up into-the sky. (3m 30s).

190. They-will-continue to-come until-you tell-him-that it-will most-likely-be unnecessary to-collect-the-class together. (J times in 2m).

191. TRANSLATE.

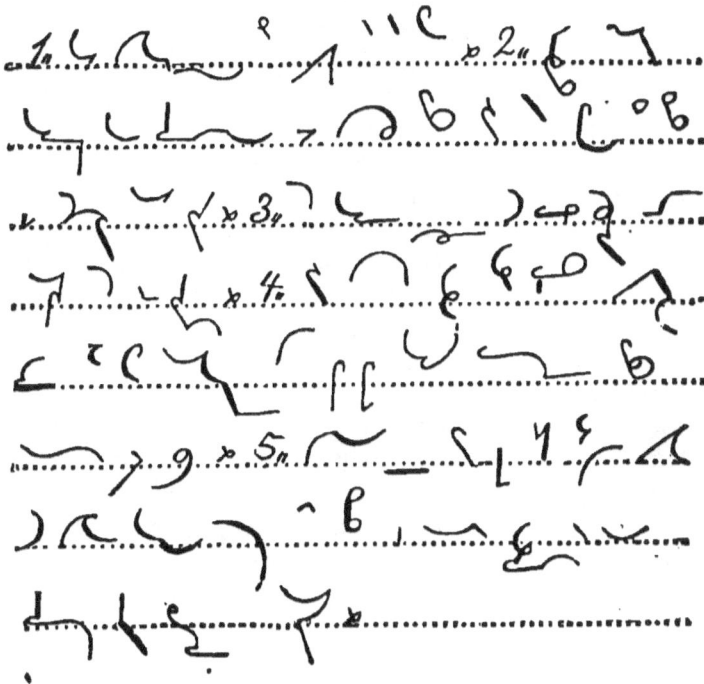

LESSON XIII.

THE R-HOOK SERIES OF DOUBLE CONSONANTS—SEC. I.

192.

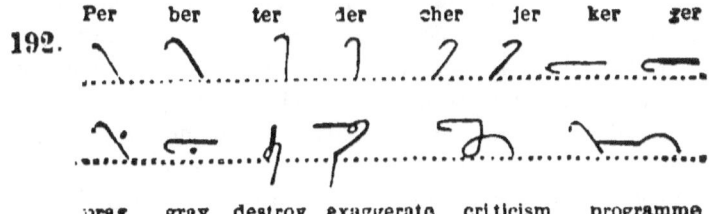

Per ber ter der cher jer ker ger

pray gray destroy exaggerate criticism programme

193. Another initial hook, written on the left of the consonant, or side opposite the l-hook, indicates the added *r* as in *pray*, or *gray*. The alphabetic letters, modified by the attachment of this hook, are denominated per, ber, ter, etc., and have the force of pe-ar, be-ar, etc. This hook is joined to all the consonants except es, ze, ar, ing, way, yea, hay, ray, and emp.

194. In order that the r-hook may be prefixed to a medial consonant, a preceding s-circle is written out of its usual position: *e. g.*, in *destroy*, the circle is placed on the left side of de in order that the r-hook may appear to be attached to te. The hook is sometimes expressed, also, by retracing a preceding consonant, as in *programme*.

195. Write, using the r-hook and vowels: Brace, breech, bribe, broil, gray, grow, brake, praise, pray, tribe, utter, acre, brawl, brow, caprice, crape, crawl, crew, cross-eyed, crow, dray, grape, grass, growl, loiter, odor, oyster, pauper, powder, prize, prose, pry, quaker, slaughter, taper, trace, trail, turmoil, ultra, Beatrice, Bertha, Grace; 1 pos. Greece, cry, creek, Greek. Without the vowels: Abbreviate, approach, appropriate, attorney, break, baker, broke, breathe, brevity, breach, bring, courage, crazy, create, creator, critic, cruel, crusade, crystal, currency decrease, democracy, depress, destroy, diagram, distress, disturb, drug, dress, drill, drink, drop, drum, drunk, educator, embrace, encourage, exaggerate, extra, extreme, criticism, proceed, trump, gradual, grasp, gravity, grocer, impress, industry, industrious, keeper, labor, laborious, ledger, liberal, lucre, ludicrous, major, maker, matrimony, microscope, mistress, Nebraska, neighbor, operate, operator, paper, parallel, precious, presence, press, pearl, prepare, pretty, precede, process (sez), produce, programme, progress, propose, prosper, provoke, redress, reproach, soldier, treason, triumph, vapor, vigor, abridge, aggregate, altar, alternate, apostrophe, April, arbitrary, alter, ardor, aristocracy, ascribe, astrology, banker, barber, beggar, betray, produce, brass, broker, broom, brush, burlesque, butcher, cathedral, charter, chemistry, cherish, chronometer, copper, courageous, courtesy, cracker, grub, crayon, crib, crimson, criticise, crook, crop, crucify, crumb, crush, crutch, cypress, deter, Deuteronomy, dexterous, dictator, digress, dipper, dream, trespass, fibre, Peter, garter, gracious, grass, grumble, harbor, Hebrew, inebriate, ingratiate, intrigue, laboratory, literary, messenger, ministry, monogram, mutter, nectar, obtrusive, patrol, pernicious, personate, poker, trustee, trap, trick, trim, tropic, trunk, Ambrose, Andrew, Edgar, Patrick; 1 pos. agree, crime, cross, daughter, draw, dream, dry, across, eager, increase, preach.

196. WORD AND PHRASE SIGNS.

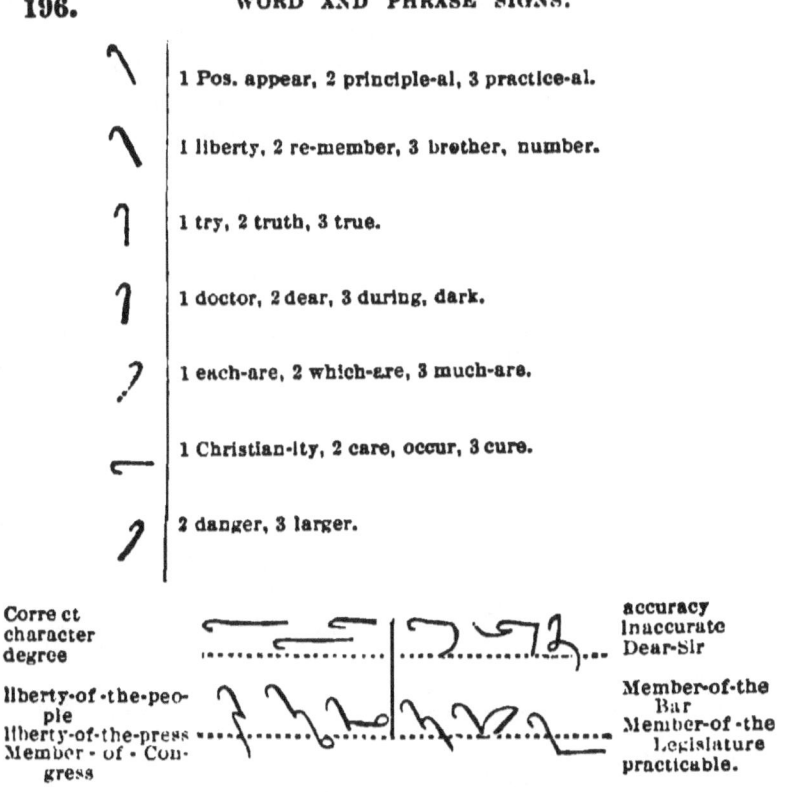

1 Pos. appear, 2 principle-al, 3 practice-al.

1 liberty, 2 re-member, 3 brother, number.

1 try, 2 truth, 3 true.

1 doctor, 2 dear, 3 during, dark.

1 each-are, 2 which-are, 3 much-are.

1 Christian-ity, 2 care, occur, 3 cure.

2 danger, 3 larger.

Correct character degree
liberty-of-the-people
liberty-of-the-press
Member-of-Congress

accuracy
Inaccurate
Dear-Sir
Member-of-the Bar
Member-of-the Legislature
practicable.

EXERCISE 13.

197. 1. He-that-takes-a wife takes care. 2. If-you-would create something, you-must-be-something. 3. Prayer is-the voice of-faith. 4. All things with-which we-deal preach to-us. 5. What vigor absence adds to-love! 6. Characters never change. 7. The-drama is-the-book of-the people. 8. The eye sees what-it brings the-power to see. 9. Genius is-the faculty of growth. 10. Life is-a comedy to-him who thinks, and-a tragedy to-him who feels. 11. The-truth of-truths is love. (2 m).

THE-CROW AND-THE PITCHER.—ÆSOP.

198. 1. A-crow, perishing for-lack of-water, sees-a pitcher, and-hoping that-it possesses some of-the liquid, flies to-it with-much joy. 2. On reaching it he-sees, to-his sorrow, that-the-water is-of so-small depth that-he-is totally unable to-reach it, so-that all-his industry avails nothing. 3. Later, he-collects as-many rocks as-it-is-possible for-him to-carry, and-with-his beak drops them slowly into-the-pitcher, until he-brings-the-water up so high that-it-is-possible for-him to-reach it, and-in-this-way saves-his life. (2 m 30 s).

199. A-member-of-the-bar, on-becoming a-Member-of-Congress, spoke in praise of-the liberty-of-the-press, and-said-that as-long-as-it published but-the simple-truth, the-liberty-of-the-people would-be in-no-danger. (5 times in 2 m).

200. TRANSLATE.

LESSON XIV.

201.   THE R-HOOK SERIES—SEC. 2.

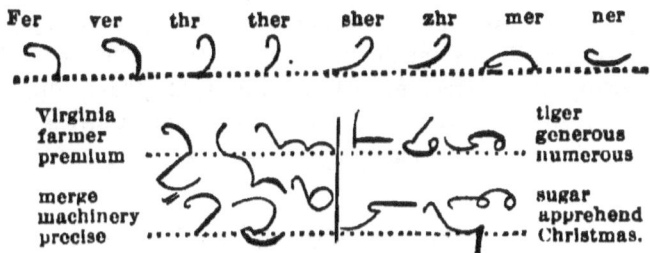

202. Since a hook can be attached to but one side of a curved letter, and since the r and l hooks are written on opposite sides of consonant stems, the natural positions of certain curves are reversed in order to render these hooks distinguishable. These curves are ef, ve, ith, and the, which, when the r-hook is prefixed, are written fer, ver, thr, and ther, as shown in the engraving, and appear like ar, way, es, and ze, with an initial hook. But these characters, it will be observed, are obtained by reversing fel, vel, thl, and thel, which is done in order that the hook may be brought to the left side. This practice gives rise to no ambiguity, since, as has been stated, the r-hook is not attached to ar, way, es, and ze.

203. To express the added ar, em and en are modified by both prefixing the hook, and thickening the stem, thus ⌒ mer, and ⌣ ner. No ambiguity results from this shading of the consonants em and en, since no hook is attached to either emp or ing.

204. In some outlines, where it cannot be conveniently joined, the hook is omitted, the shaded em simply being used in lieu of mer, as in *farmer*.

205. Write: Rumor, tremor, Homer, energy, dinner, banner, exhonorate, lunar, over, farmer, generous, numerous, tanner, merge, offer, philosopher, phrase, camphor, Christopher, Francis, Frank, average, Denver, favor, oversight, Friday, silver, traverse, leisure, measure, pressure, treasure, censure, exposure, machinery, aniversary, diverge, diverse, livery, manœuver, Luther, Lutheran, dishonor, perverse, thresh, throng, verb, verge, verse, Oliver, Virginia, wager, Arthur, Bertram, Oscar, Frank, Roger, Victor, treacherous, favorite, proverb, tributary, gather, sheriff, umbrella, repress, slipper, spider, sugar (shay), tiger, tragedy, tragic, traitor, probate, problem, profess, professor, prolong, propriety, recur, prairie, preface, premier, premise, premium, primary, prior. Vocalize, throw; 1 pos. authorize, authority, crisis (sez), decree, former, fever, free, preside, prime, minor, oppress, oppressive, precise (sez), price, Christmas; 3 pos. abstruse, address, adverse, affirm, apprehend, apprehensive, presume, scatter, assure, grew, troop.

206. WORD AND PHRASE SIGNS.

1 Pos. author, 2 three, 3 through.

1 either, 2 their, there, they-are, 3 other.

1 Mr., mere, remark-able, 2 more, mercy, 3 humor.

1 near, nor, honor, 2 manner, 3 owner.

From every, very pleasure

in-reference-to in-respect-to honorable

therefore Thursday Friday

commercial University San Francisco.

EXERCISE 14.

207. 1. He-remarks to-his brother-members that-to encourage such-pleasures is-in-a-high degree dangerous to-every-principle of-Christian-liberty. 2. The-doctor's practice in-San-Francisco gradually increases, and-his skill has-no parallel. 3. The-author of-the ludicrous "Dream of-the Major's Daughter" exaggerates beyond-measure in-speaking-of-the-crimes of-war. (1 m 15 s)

THE-DOG AND-THE SHADOW.—ÆSOP.

208. 1. A-dog crossing-a bridge over-a-creek with-a piece of-flesh in-his mouth, sees his own shadow in-the-water, and-takes-it for that of-some-other dog, with-a piece-of game double his own in size. 2. He-therefore drops his own piece, and-furiously attacks-the-other dog with-the view of-taking-his larger piece from-him. 3. He-thus looses both; that-which he-grasps for in-the-water, because-it-was-a shadow; and-his own, because-the-creek washes it-away. (2 m).

209. 1. So sad, so fresh, the-days that-are no-more. 2. You-arrive at truth through poetry, and-I arrive at poetry through truth. 3. Lay a-bridge of-silver for-a flying enemy. 4. What-is becoming is honorable, and-what-is honorable is becoming. 5. The-eyes of-other people are-the eyes that ruin us. 6. Wise judges are-we of-each-other. (1 m 30 s).

210. It-is-the-more remarkable, for I-supposed that-he-had too-much honor to-be author-of-such-a rumor as-this in-reference-to Oliver the-philosopher. (10 times in 3 m).

211. TRANSLATE.

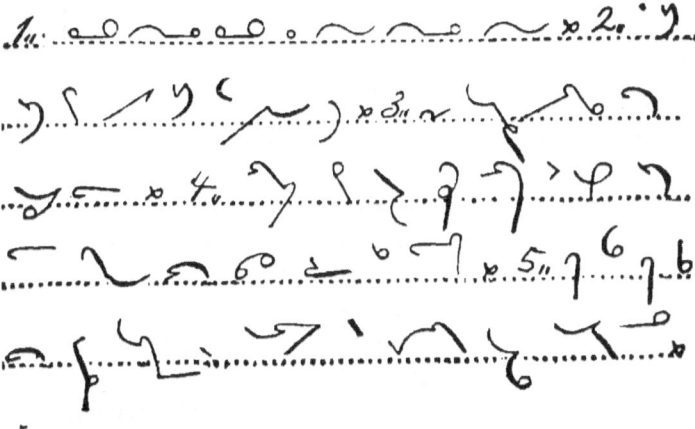

LESSON XV.

212. THE TRIPLE-CONSONANT SERIES.

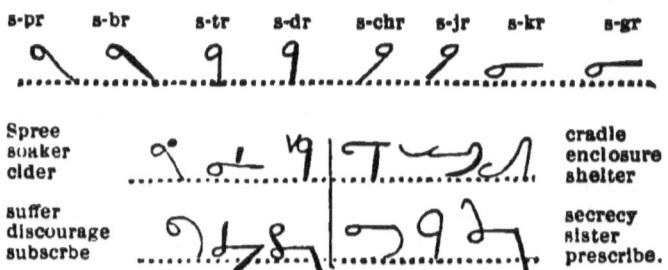

Spree, soaker, cider, suffer, discourage, subscrbe, cradle, enclosure, shelter, secrecy, sister, prescribe.

213. When the s-circle is to be prefixed to per, the hook is omitted, and the circle written on the r-hook side of the consonant; thus, the character *sper* has the force of es-pe-ar, as in *spree*.

214. The triple consonant *sper* is more easily written than though the circle were placed within the hook; and it will not be mistaken for *spe* simply, since in *sper* the circle is placed on the opposite side of the consonant. All other *straight* stems of the r-hook series are modified in the same manner to express a preceding *s*, as in *soaker* and *cider*.

215. But when the circle is to be prefixed to *fer*, it must be written within the hook, as in *suffer*; otherwise it would be written *ser*, and have the force of es-ar, instead of es-ef-ar. The same principle holds true of all curved double consonants, *ver*, *ther*, etc.

216. In the outlines for a few such words as *discourage* and *subscribe*, where it is inconvenient to write the r-hook, it is entirely omitted, r being readily supplied from the context.

217. Write: String, spring, struck, strong, scourge, scribe, secrecy, sober, sister, suffer, discourage, discriminate, disgrace, subscribe, sacrifice, scrub, separate, skirmish, strap, stress, stretch, succor, supercede, superstitious, supper, supremacy,

TRIPLE CONSONANTS. 67

supreme; 1 pos. strike, prescribe, scream; 3 pos. scrap, scratch, strew. Vocalize, strow, stray, streak. Using both the l and r hooks: agreeable, brutal, clamor, clatter, flatter, flavor, proclaim, travel, triangle, trouble, verbal, calibre, chronicle, clapper, clever, clover, cradle, flutter, girdle, glitter, grapple, inclosure, perplex, propel, shelter, trifle, triple, tropical, scruple, struggle.

218. WORD AND PHRASE SIGNS.

Merciful
mortgage
neighborhood

proper-ty
universal
New-Hampshire

West-Virginia
disappear
disagree

express
surprise
suppress

overwhelm
probable-ly
probability

forgive
North-America
South-America

everlasting
strength, external
as-it-were

Scripture, describe
secure
such-are, 3 such were

EXERCISE 15.

219. 1. Their-sisters in-South-America subscribe for-the University papers published in New-Hampshire and-West-Virginia. 2. The-philosopher expresses surprise at-the-large number of-sacrifices which-the Scriptures describe. 3. America, in-her dealings, is-fair and-honorable, and-has-no troubles with-other peoples. 4. Such-were-their brutal clamors for-more of-the silver treasure, that-we-had-to suffer, as-it-were, a-cruel scourge. (1m 30s).

220. THE-CEDAR TREE AND-THE BRAMBLE.—ÆSOP.

1. A-cedar tree, bragging, says-to-the bramble, "You-are useful for-nothing at-all, but in-all-places people use me for houses and-stables." 2. The-bramble answers: "You poor thing, if-you-would-but remember-the axes and-saws which-are soon-to hew you to pieces, you-would-have-reason to wish that-you-were-a bramble also, as-I-am. 3. Riches bring cares. (1m 30s).

4. The-devil can cite Scripture for-his-purpose. 5. Know how sublime it-is to-suffer and-be strong. 6. All cruelty springs from weakness.

221. They-will-set out on-the fourth Thursday of-April, and-travel from-North to-South-America for-pleasure merely. (15 times in 3m).

222. TRANSLATE.

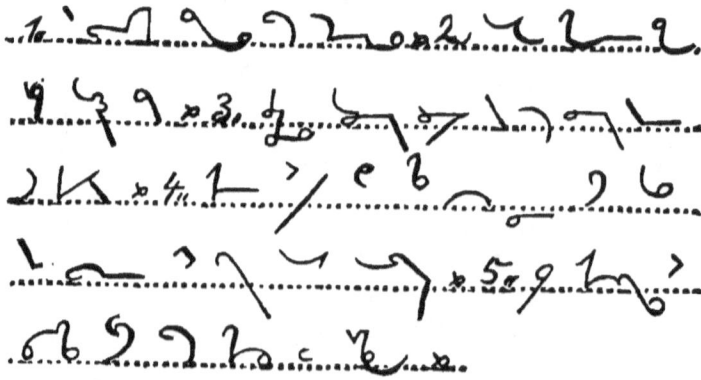

REMARK.—The learner is liable to confound these two hooks, writing *l* for *r* and *r* for *l*. A mnemonic aid commonly made use of is the following: The proper side of the consonant stem for placing the *l-hook* is indicated by bending the index finger of the left hand; and for placing the *r-hook*, by bending the same finger of the right hand. It will be observed, too, that not only is the right hand (R-hand) used more frequently than the left (L-hand), but the *r-hook* is used more frequently than the *l*.

NOTE.—To the professional stenographer a knowledge of spelling is absolutely indispensable. So many good Short-hand writers fail to hold a situation on account of deficiency in this much neglected art, that it is a matter of prudence, if your knowledge is imperfect in this regard, to begin improving it at once. Learn to spell words with your *pen* rather than your *tongue*. *Written spelling* is more important to the reporter, and quite distinct from *oral spelling*.

LESSON XVI.

THE REL-HOOK, AND THE ASPIRATE TICK AND DOT.

223.

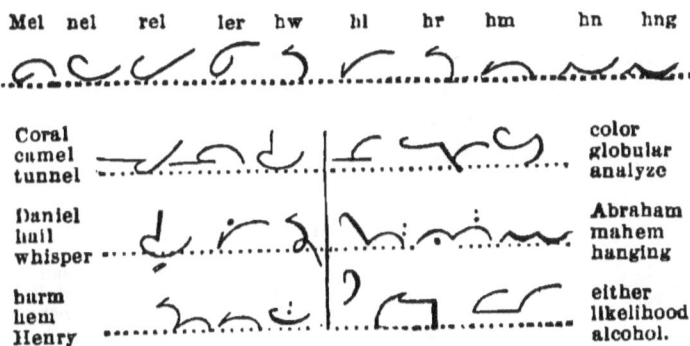

224. The liquid *l* occurs so frequently in connection with ray, em, and en, as in *choral*, *camel*, and *tunnel*, that it has been found expedient to denote the double sounds rl, ml, and nl, by attaching a large initial hook to the stems ray, em, and en, the double letters thus obtained being named *mel*, *nel*, and *rel*.

225. A large initial hook attached to lay signifies that ar is to be added, the character *ler* being equivalent to lay-ar, as in *color*.

226. Write: Animal, tunnel, signal, penal, color, diagonal, finally, family, nominal, original, Colorado, relish, paternal, relic, globular, criminal, colonel, scholar, necessarily, centennial, abdominal, analyze, arsenal (ar), autumnal, barrel, canal, chronology, gallery, jocular, millennial, millennium, polar, sentinel, spinal, relate, temporal (emp), tribunal, venal, Daniel. *1 pos.* collar, rely, release, reliance. *3 pos.* plural, analogy.

THE ASPIRATE TICK.

227. A short initial tick, derived from hay, signifying the aspirate *h*, and so written as to form an acute angle with the consonant to which it is joined, is prefixed to way, el, ar, en, em, ing, kay and gay, as in *hale*, or *whisper*.

228. Write: Hang, harp, harm, holiday, whisper, whiskey, hell, hem, homicide, wheel, whip, whistle, hair; 1 pos. horse. Vocalize, hare, heal, whale, hum, hale, hall, hire, hollow.

THE ASPIRATE DOT.

229. Hay, when medial, sometimes fails to make a good angle by its junction with other letters; as, for instance, when it occurs before em. In such cases the aspirate is signified by a small dot written just before the vowel, as in *Abraham, mayhem.*

Using the dot: Abraham, Henry, mayhem. Omitting the dot: hither, likelihood, alcohol, adhere.

230. WORD AND PHRASE SIGNS.

Real, rely roll, rail rule

reality reliable unless

railroad railway-car behalf

relinquish only Lord Jesus Christ.

231. EXERCISE 16.

1. A-thing-of beauty is-a joy forever. 2. Custom is-the-law of fools. 3. Faith is-necessary to victory. 4. Fear has-many eyes. 5. Gaiety is-the soul's health; sadness is-its poison. 6. Her ample page rich with-the spoils of-time. 7. For hope is but-the dream of-those-that wake. 8. Unto-the-pure all things are pure. 9. Innocence is always unsuspicious. 10. Kings ought-to-be kings in-all things. 11. Knowledge is power. 12. Laugh if-you-are wise. 13. And-he that-lives to-live-forever never fears dying. 14. To-live-long, it-is-necessary to-live slowly. 15. Study to-be quiet. (2m 30s).

232. While-the railway-car is traveling-to Denver, he-thinks-it-possible for-the colonel to-ride there on horse-back. (15 times in 3m).

233. TRANSLATE.

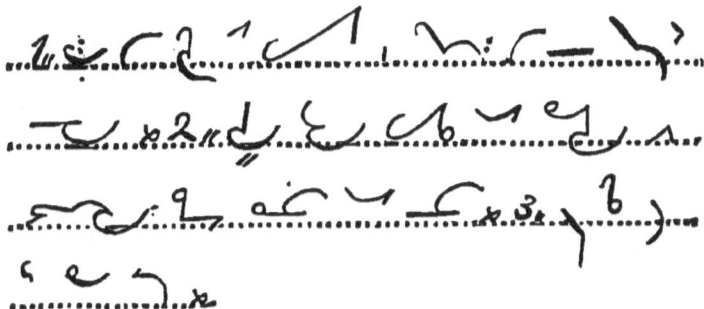

LESSON XVII.

234. THE W-HOOK.

wel		wen
wer		sail
wem		wail
quail		swear
quorum		Wednesday
swim		wilderness

235. A small initial hook, representing the consonant w, is attached to lay, ray, em, and en, the characters thus formed being named wel, wer, wem, and wen.

236. The w-hook is derived from the coalescent semi-circle ⊂ weh, which, when prefixed to these consonants, is so adapted as to form a hook. The w-hook differs essentially from the r, l, and rel hook series. The w-hook itself, after the analogy of the s-circle, denotes the consonant way; e. g., in sail and wail, both the circle and hook are read before lay. Whereas, in the other series above named, the hook itself does not represent l or r, but is simply a modification of the consonant stem to denote that one or the other of these liquids is to be *added;* e. g., the character ⌒ *acre* is not read *rake,* as it would be did the hook itself, which is formed first, denote *r.* The w-hook is itself the sign for *w,* while in the double consonant (the l, r, and rel hook) series, each hooked letter is an indivisible character representing *pl, pr, ler,* etc.

237. Write: Quill, quire, quorum, swim, ware, wealth, Wednesday, welfare, wilderness, wolf, worm, Edwin, Walter, William, work, worth, worthy, well, willing, window, one, wear, warm, swear, acquire, beware. Vocalize, choir, weary, quail, wall, wine, wool.

238. WORD AND PHRASE SIGNS.

1 Pos. we-are, 2 where, 3 aware.

1 while, we-will, 2 well, 3 awhile.

1 with-me, 2 we-may, with-him, 3 with-whom.

1 anywhere, inquire-y, 2 nowhere, 3 unaware.

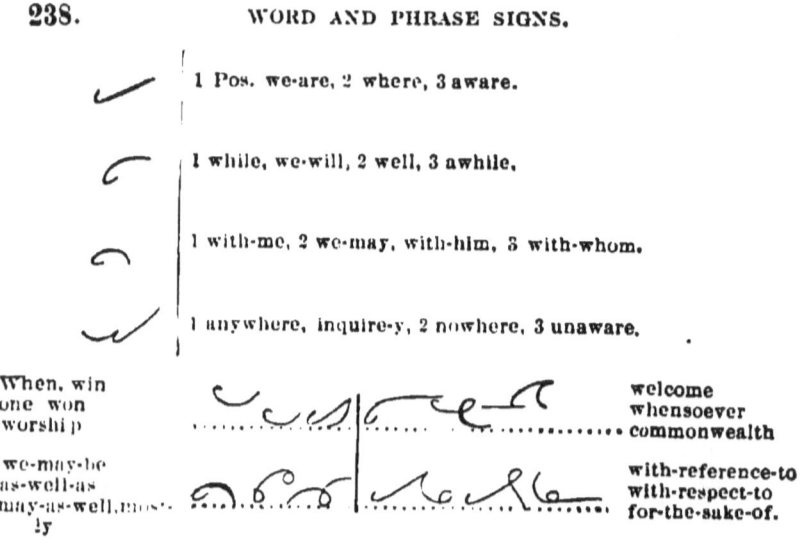

When, win, one won, worship — welcome, whensoever, commonwealth

we-may-be, as-well-as, may-as-well, mostly — with-reference-to, with-respect-to, for-the-sake-of.

EXERCISE 17.

239. 1. Necessity does everything well. 2. We-are near waking when-we dream that-we dream. 3. When-you-give, give with joy and-smiling. 4. Hope is-a-willing slave. 5. They laugh that win. 6. Law should-be-like death, which spares no-one. 7. Love may hope, where reason would-despair. 8. The-scholarly colonel gives-us reliable news with-reference-to the Colorado railroads. 9. The-prize the-teacher offers for-a really correct exercise is-a family horse of bay color, and-every pupil should try to win-it if-possible. 10. There-is-no harm in-having-a holiday once-in-a while, but it-would-be well if-the scholar should-take-them only rarely. (2 m 30 s).

THE HARE AND-THE TORTOISE.—ÆSOP.

240. 1. The hare one-day laughs at-the stubby legs and-slow pace of-the tortoise. 2. The-latter, laughing, said, "Though-you travel like-a railway-car I-will-win in-a-race with-you." 3. The hare, deeming what-she affirms to-be-simply-impossible, agrees to-the proposal. 4. They-also agree that-the fox shall choose the-race-track, and-fix the-goal. 5. On Wednesday, the-day which-the fox selects for-the-race, they-set out together. 6. The-tortoise never pauses at-all, but-travels on-with-a slow and-uniform pace until she finally reaches the-tree. 7. The hare, relying on-his original quickness, has-no-anxiety as-to-the outcome of-the-race, but leisurely eats his dinner by-the wayside and-falls asleep. 8. Finally, waking up, and-moving quickly as-possible, he-sees the-tortoise already at-the goal, and-quietly dozing there. (3 m).

241. Beware of-sitting by-the railway-car window while-we-are crossing over-the dangerous bridge. (12 times in 2 m).

242. TRANSLATE.

LESSON XVIII.

THE F-HOOK.

243.

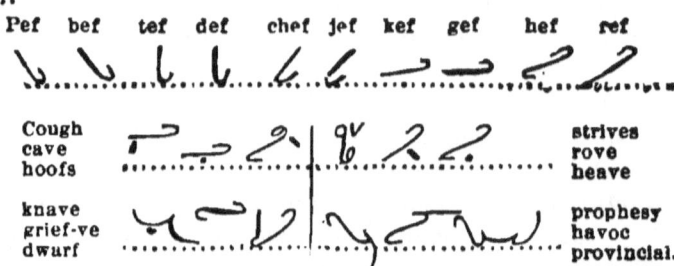

244. A final hook, signifying ef or ve, is written on the s-circle side of all straight letters: e. g. the character *kef* signifies kay-ef, as in *cough*, and kay-ve, as in *cave*. A following s-circle is written within the hook, as in *hoofs* or *strives*.

245. Using the f-hook and vowels: Cuff, cough, beer, cave, Jove, devout, crave, hive. Without vowels: Bereave, beverage, cuff, bluff, cavalry, cavil, deaf, dwarf, gave, glove, gruff, incentive, lithograph, octave, primitive, prophesy, havoc, province, provincial, puff, river, roof, rough, relief (rel), scoff, sensitive, staff, strife, strive, tough, David, Stephen;] pos. drive, grieve, grief.

246. *Rem.* The fact that either one of any two cognate sounds may be represented by the same sign without danger of ambiguity, has been fully shown in the case of the s and z circle. The same principle applies in the case of the f-hook, which is used for either of the two sounds, *f* and *v*, without ambiguity, as in the sentence, "They may well ⸺, considering their cause of ⸺." The student will observe that the f-hook, which is always written on the s-circle side of consonants, appears on the left side of hay and ray, as in *rove* and *heave*. As this hook *is attached to straight letters only,* the alphabetic ef and ve must be used whenever a curve immediately precedes them. E. g. *knave* is written with the full-length en-ve, since the hook cannot be used for ve after the curve en.

247.   WORD AND PHRASE SIGNS.

1 Pos. ought-to-have, it-ought-to-have, 2 whatever, 3 out-of, it-would-have.

1 which-ought-to-have, 2 whichever, which-have, 3 which-would-have.

1 such-ought-to-have, 2 such-have, 3 such-would-have.

1 perfect, 2 proof, prove, 3 approve.

1 each-will-have, 2 which-will-have, 3 much-will-have.

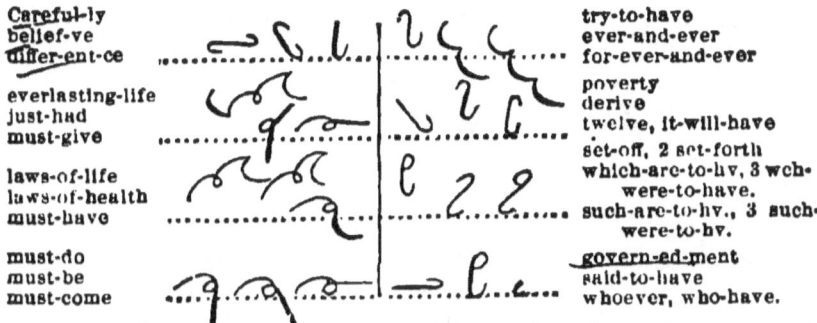

Careful-ly
belief-ve
differ-ent-ce

everlasting-life
just-had
must-give

laws-of-life
laws-of-health
must-have

must-do
must-be
must-come

try-to-have
ever-and-ever
for-ever-and-ever

poverty
derive
twelve, it-will-have

set-off, 2 set-forth
which-are-to-hv, 3 wch-were-to-have.
such-are-to-hv., 3 such-were-to-hv.

govern-ed-ment
said-to-have
whoever, who-have.

EXERCISE 18.

248   THE WIDOW AND-THE SHEEP.—ÆSOP.

1. A-poor widow had-one solitary sheep. 2. At shearing-time, wishing-to-take its fleece and-to avoid paying out-a-very large sum of-money, she-took-it with her shears so unskillfully, that-with-the fleece she-took-the flesh. 3. The-sheep, writhing because-of-the injury, said, "Why do-you do me so-much harm? 4. What-weight does-my-life add to-the wool? 5. If-you-wish my flesh,

there-is-the butcher who-will kill me in-a trice. 6. But if-you-wish to-take my fleece only, there-is-the shearer, who-will shear me and-do no harm." 7. Much loss may-be-caused by-making too-small an-outlay. (2m).

249. You-should obey the-laws-of-health if-you-would-have relief now; and-be governed by wise proverbs, if-you-would-have everlasting-life. (8 times in 2m).

250.   TRANSLATE.

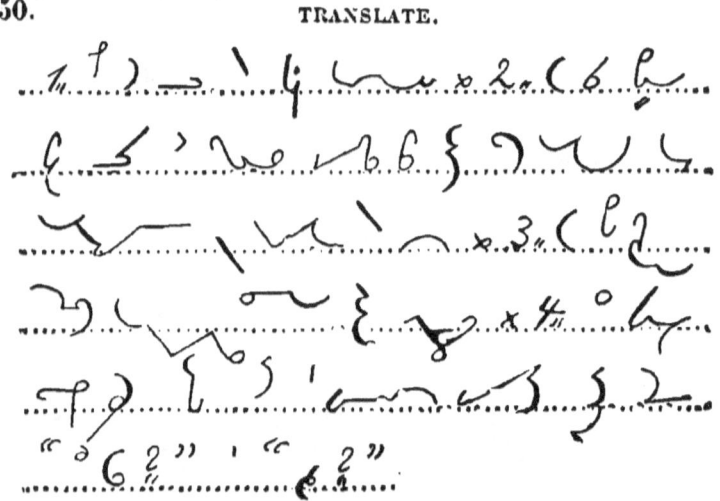

NOTE.—Most pupils make the light lines heavier than is proper, the result of too much pressure of the pen upon the paper. It is an excellent plan to cultivate lightness of touch by frequent practice in writing the thin stems as fine as possible, executing them rapidly, touching the paper very lightly with the pen.

THE TYPE-WRITER.—Type-writing is much more rapid, and in various ways far superior to pen work. A knowledge of this art itself is very valuable, and has become entirely indispensable to the professional Stenographer. The Private Secretary is almost invariably required to make use of a writing machine in preparing transcripts and copies. He is, moreover, expected to be familiar with its operation before he accepts a situation, and skill in manipulating it should, if practicable, be gained while the course in Stenography is being taken.

LESSON XIX.

251. THE N-HOOK.

Pen ben ten den chen jen ken gen hen ren

Tone, roan, twine

queen, Eugene, adjourn

abstinence, economy, brain

sustain, barbarian, stricken

chagrin, cistern, strain

tangible, Unitarian, sanguine.

252. Another final hook, signifying *n*, is annexed to both straight and curved letters. When joined to straight stems, it is written on the side opposite the f-hook, as in *tone* or *roan*.

253. Vocalize: Cane, chain, dawn, dine, pain, rainbow, stain, tone, canopy, acorn, bane, bean, bone, dean, deign, drone, pan, pin, pine, twine, reign, Eugene, Jane, Jean; 1 pos. keen, coin, queen. Without vowels: Again, been, can, run, stone, ten, gain, abandon, abstain, abstinence, chaplain, adjourn, branch, bunch, burn, corn, cotton, deacon, denounce, detain, libertine, discipline, disdain, economy, kitchen, Latin, mechanic, mourn, obtain, train, candy, ordain, organ (ar), origin, pagan, reckon, retain, scorn, southern, drench, planet, Spanish, sudden, sustain, taken, turn, obstinate, torn, vacancy, beacon, propound, denote, wagon, Michigan, Oregon (ar), banish, barbarian, barn, beckon, bench, blown, born, bounty, canton, canvass, stricken, captain, cavern, chagrin, chicken, chin, cistern, county, cunning, dainty, den, din, disjoin, expunge, foreign, gentile, glen, groan, grown, hinge, hurricane, laconic, maiden, marine, mitten, panic, pen, pinch, plunge, retrench, ribbon, sanguine, skin, span, sponge, strain, surgeon, tangible, tenacious, tinge, ton, trench, Unitarian, virgin, waken, weapon, wrench, Austin, Conrad, Dan, John, Blanch; 1 pos. spine, tin, join, enjoin, chronic; 3 pos. attune, attain, brown, June, town, spoon.

254. WORD AND PHRASE SIGNS.

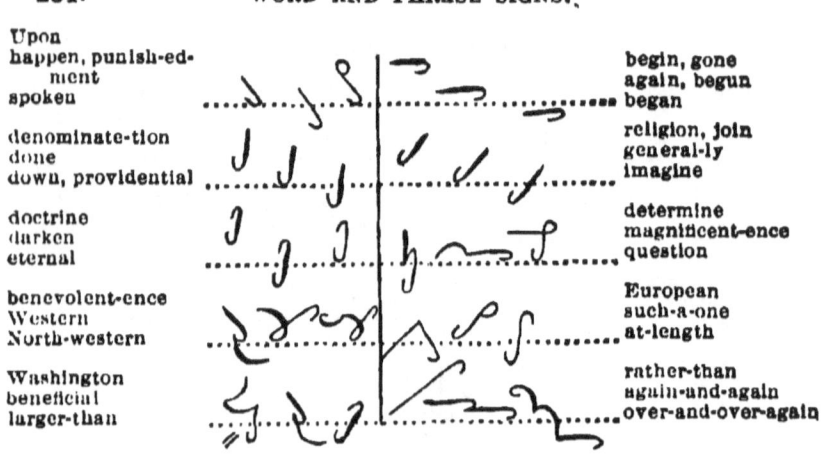

Upon
happen, punish-ed-
 ment
spoken

denominate-tion
done
down, providential

doctrine
darken
eternal

benevolent-ence
Western
North-western

Washington
beneficial
larger-than

begin, gone
again, begun
began

religion, join
general-ly
imagine

determine
magnificent-ence
question

European
such-a-one
at-length

rather-than
again-and-again
over-and-over-again

EXERCISE 19.

255. 1. Pain may-be-said to-follow pleasure as-its shadow. 2. Peace is rarely denied to-the peaceful. 3. Pity is akin to-love. 4. Pity is love when-grown into excess. 5. Prayer is-to religion what thinking is-to philosophy. 6. To-pray is-to-make religion. 7. He-that-has-no cross deserves no-crown. 8. The-Bible is-a-window in-this prison of hope, through which-we look into-eternity. (1 m 30 s).

256. It-has-been spoken again-and-again by-the chaplain that-the-doctrine of-the Christian-religion is-that-life is eternal, rather-than-a-brief span only. (7 times in 2 m).

CAUTION.—Be careful to make your hooks and S-circles quite small. Avoid the error beginners commonly make of getting these on the wrong side of the stem. Vowel word-signs should be short, and all "ticks" used in phraseography both short and light.

THE N-HOOK. 79

257. TRANSLATE.

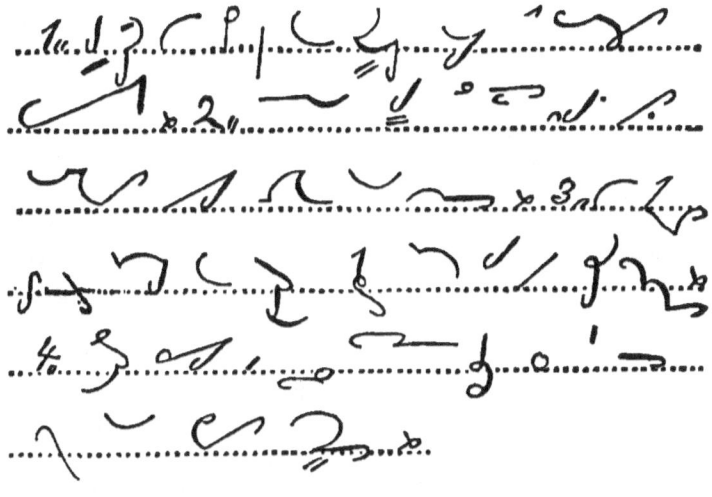

LESSON XX.

THE N-HOOK—CONTINUED.

258.

Fen ven thn then esn zen shen zhen len arn men nen wayn yen

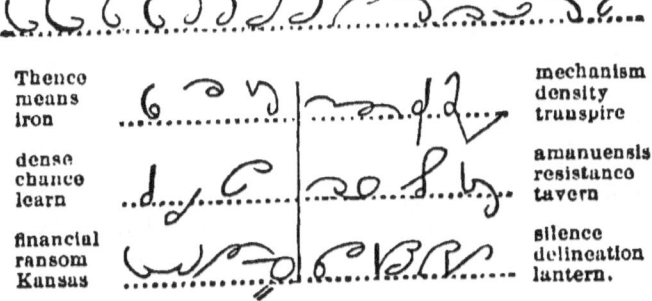

Thence
means
iron

dense
chance
learn

financial
ransom
Kansas

mechanism
density
transpire

amanuensis
resistance
tavern

silence
delineation
lantern.

259. Since a hook can be conveniently written only within, or following the direction of curves, but one final hook can be joined to these letters. This is properly chosen to represent n, which occurs much more frequently than f and v.

260. Vocalize: Lean, loan, iron, noun, Ethan, Julian, Adaline. Without vowels: Man, main, known, none, Maine, cannon, coffin, cognomen, dominion, earn (ar), examine, fancy, finish, infancy, arrange (ar), Italian, learn, lengthen, machine, maintain, manage, manager, minute, saloon, Monday, monarch, monotonous, Roman, season, sermon (ar), situation, menace, then, specimen, vanity, vanish, villain, vain, anonymous, German, **French, London,** admonish, affront, almanac, amanuensis, amen, arraign (ar), battalion, brilliancy, clemency, delineation, diminish, diminution, diminutive, domain, feminine, finance, financial, **fringe, frown, fun,** infringe, lantern, launch, lone, lunatic, lunch, minimum, monopolize, monopoly, moon, muslin, ocean, omen, orphan, outline, permanence, million (mcl), phenomenon, Prussian, raven, refine, refrain, shun, summon, sunshine, tavern, thin, throne, tuition, urn (ar), van, varnish, vein, venom, vine, violin, workman, Aaron, Allen, Alonzo, Benjamin, Franklin, Jonathan, Napoleon, Nathan, Orlando, Solomon, Helen, Josephine, Lillian, Susan. 1 pos. men, even, evening, often, line, mine, mean, meaning, fine, shine, thine; 3 pos. than, noon.

261. When the n-hook is attached to curves, a following s-circle is expressed by being written within the hook, as in *thence*, or *means*.

262. Write, fence, lance, opulence, pestilence, ransom, renounce, patience, excellence, thence, violence, France, silence, lonesome, specimens.

263. At the end of words, this consonant is expressed after straight letters by locating the s-circle on the n-hook side, as in *dense*, or *chance*.

264. Write: Cadence, credence, decadence, glance, guidance, occurrence, bronze, intense, prince, residence, resistance, semblance, tense, distance, pretense, expense, trance, **trans¦tory,** vengeance, dense, instance, dispense, abundance, **extensive,** eloquence (el), disdains, detains, Lawrence, Kansas; 3 pos. chance, dance, towns, appliance.

THE N-HOOK. 81

265. But the circle is written within the hook when medial, although annexed to a straight letter, as in *mechanism*. In *density*, however, and a few words having similar outlines, the hook is implied by the manner in which the circle is written. The writing of the medial *n*, when its hook cannot be easily expressed, is often entirely omitted, as in *transpire*, this consonant in such cases being readily supplied from the context.

266. Write: Pennsylvania, transpose, transpire, organism, mechanism, Wisconsin, density, intrinsic, transverse, minstrel, transcribe.

267. WORD AND PHRASE SIGNS.

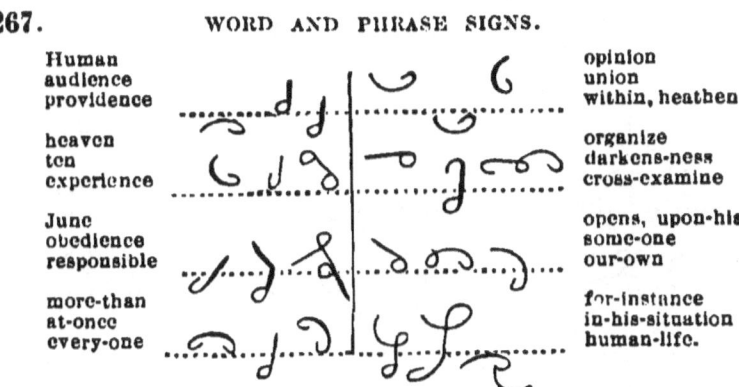

Human
audience
providence

heaven
ten
experience

June
obedience
responsible

more-than
at-once
every-one

opinion
union
within, heathen

organize
darkens-ness
cross-examine

opens, upon-his
some-one
our-own

for-instance
in-his-situation
human-life.

268. EXERCISE 20.

1. To obtain excellence in-any language requires much study-and patience; especially is-this true of Latin and-Greek. 2. She receives-lessons in French every Monday, and-in Spanish every Thursday. 3. That-she-may thoroughly learn her lessons, she-writes every-line over-and-over-again. 4. She will-make use of-these languages in-her European travels. 5. In-his-situation, he-would-be-likely-to improve his health the-more by sailing to-London, rather-than going all-the-way in-a-wagon. (1 m 30 s).

269. 1. Men are April when-they woo, December when-they wed. 2. All of heaven we-have below. 3. Nothing maintains its bloom forever; age succeeds to-age. 4. To-err is human; to-forgive, divine. 5. Many-men know how to-flatter, few-men know how to-praise. 6. Learn-to-labor and-to wait. 7. No-man
6

flatters the-woman he-truly loves. 8. Love is-a-reality which-is born in-the fairy regions of romance. 9. Shallow men believe in luck; strong men believe in-cause-and-effect. (1 m 45 s).

270. Every-one who begins the-study of human-life will-believe more-than ever-before in Providential guidance. (5 times in 1 m).

271.   TRANSLATE.

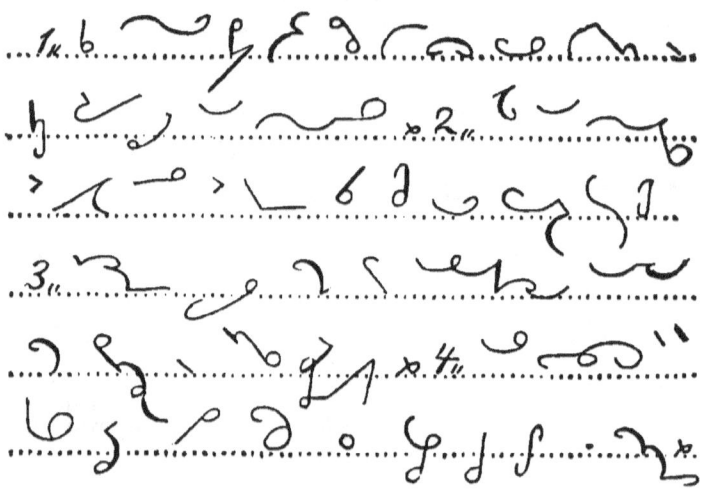

LESSON XXI.

THE SHUN-HOOK.

272.

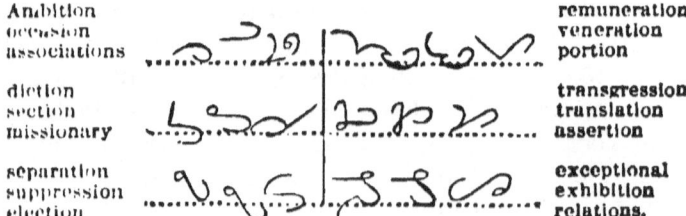

Ambition	remuneration
occasion	veneration
associations	portion
diction	transgression
section	translation
missionary	assertion
separation	exceptional
suppression	exhibition
election	relations.

THE SHUN-HOOK.

273. A large final hook, corresponding in size with the rel-hook, is used to denote the frequent endings *tion*, *cion*, *sion*, etc. This hook is written within curves, as in *ambition*, and on the s-circle side of straight letters, as in *occasion*. Like the hook for *f* and *v*, this also, as shown by the examples just given, represents two cognate sounds, viz. *shn* and *zhn*.

274. Vocalize: Emotion; 1 pos. auction. Without vowels: Action, attention, abbreviation, animation, dissipation, declamation, definition, depression, dissension, designation, desolation, devotion, discussion, elevation, emigration, evasion, expedition, foundation, impression, indignation, intimation, rational, irrational (ar), limitation, motion, locomotion, nation, notation, occupation, omission, oration (ar), presumption, probation, prosecution, profession, provision, repetition, revision, selection, session, submission, association, acclamation, aggregation, ammunition, crucifixion, promotion, dictation, dimension, amputation (emp), ascension, aspiration, assassination, assimilation, celebration, coalition, decapitation, delusion, digression, discrimination, division, elongation, emulation, erection, erudition, evolution, exclamation, exertion, exhortation, expectation, exportation, extermination, exultation, inflammation, invasion, involution, isolation, lamentation, location, negotiation, nutrition, observation, option, penetration, pension, perpetration, persecution, petition, population, preservation, prevention, profusion, progression, prolongation, recrimination, remuneration, resolution, restoration, restriction, resurrection, salutation, separation, solution, subscription, supervision, termination, transgression, translation, veneration, violation, volition; 1 pos. creation, edition, mission, missionary, occasion, vision, caution, option, alleviation; 3 pos. addition, approbation, dissolution, passion, reputation, allusion.

275. When the straight letter to which this hook is attached is preceded by a hook, circle, or other consonant sign, on the s-circle side, it will be found more convenient to strike the shun-hook on the side opposite, as in *education*, or *section*.

276. Write: Election, exception, execution, education, exclusion, exhibition, fraction, induction, intoxication, invocation, obligation, plantation, restitution, portion, proportion, distribution, assertion, vegetation, reception, reflection, relation, section, station,

84 REPORTING STYLE OF SHORT-HAND.

adoration, suspicion, recollection, abduction, adjudication, adoption, affection, benediction, benefaction, classification, dejection, distraction, edification, expiration, exploration, explosion, faction, friction, infection, fiction, projection, seclusion, specification, substitution, vacation, variation, visitation; 1 pos. diction, dictionary; 3 pos. agitation, application, attraction, elocution (el), suppression, avocation.

277.   WORD-SIGNS.

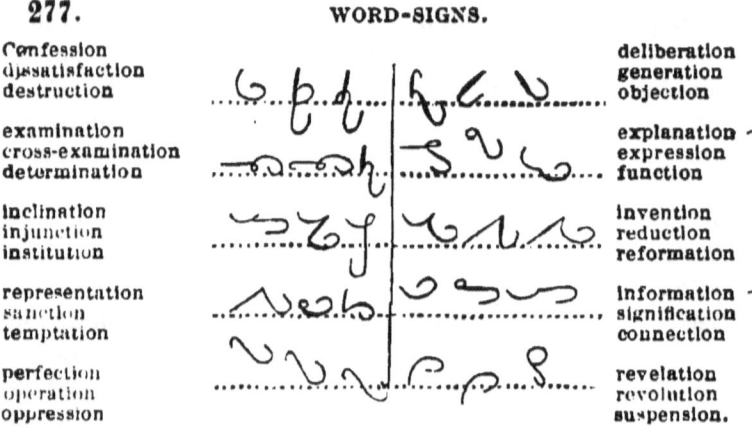

Confession	deliberation
dissatisfaction	generation
destruction	objection
examination	explanation
cross-examination	expression
determination	function
inclination	invention
injunction	reduction
institution	reformation
representation	information
sanction	signification
temptation	connection
perfection	revelation
operation	revolution
oppression	suspension.

EXERCISE 21.

278. 1. The-two offices of-memory are collection and-distribution. 2. Whatever is popular deserves attention. 3. I-know no-manner of-speaking so offensive as-that of-giving praise and-closing it with-an-exception. 4. The-only-things in-which-we can-be-said to-have-any property are our-actions. 5. Strong reasons make strong-actions. 6. We ask advice, but we-mean approbation. 7. Affectation discovers sooner what one is than-it-makes-known what one would fain appear to-be. 8. No decking sets-forth anything so-much-as affection. 9. We-are-never like angels till-our passion dies. 10. Charity is-a-wish for-a-perfect education. 11. All-is holy where devotion kneels. 12. Education is-the-chief defense of nations. 13. Love is-the piety of-the affections. 14. Take away ambition and-vanity, and-where-will-be your heroes and-patriots? (2 m 30 s).

279. The-lawyer raises objections to-the cross-examination for-the-reason-that-the witness, in-making his explanation of-the invention, gives-information as-to-his-own profession, which-has-no-relation to-his examination-in-chief. (3 times in 1 m).

280. TRANSLATE.

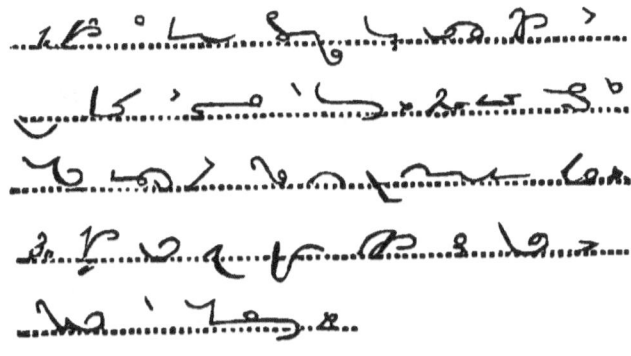

LESSON XXII.

281. THE S-SHUN AND INITIAL N HOOKS.

Civilization transitions dispensation		cessation imposition demonstration
enslave inscribe inseparable		pronounce prudence worn
economical woman, 1 pos. women trunce		paragraph prefer reference
transmission qualification furniture		traffic venerable graphic.

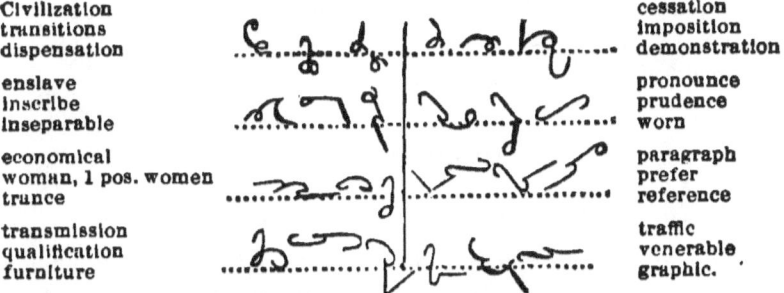

282. The syllables denoted by the shun-hook, when they occur after an s-circle, are expressed by continuing the stroke until a small hook is formed on the side opposite, as in *civilization*. The plural is formed by writing a circle within the hook, as in *transitions*.

283. Write: Deposition, dispositions, accession, physician, position, positions, propositions, sensation, supposition, civilization, imposition, cessation, exposition, procession, requisition, succession, vexation, dispensation; 1 pos. decision, opposition, precision, acquisition; 3 pos. accusation, transition, possession, possessions.

THE INITIAL N-HOOK.

284. The prefixes in, en, and un, when followed by a circle and curve with which the alphabetic ⌒en would not form a convenient juncture, are denoted by a similar hook, as in *enslave*. This is also used in connection with the triple consonant series, as in *inscribe*, or *inseparable*.

285. Using the proper initial and final hooks: Curtain, drain, drove, engrave, explain, grain, graphic, grave, matron, patron, plain, plenty, pronounce, prudence, utterance, restrain, train, venerable, worn, decline, economical, tribune, incline, woman, criterion, demonstration, furniture, paragraph, prefer, reference, transgress, transmission; 1 pos. qualification, women, clean, cleave, clime, green; 3 pos. transcribe, crown, drown, plan, traffic, administration.

286. PHRASE SIGNS.

In-some	In-consideration
In-as-many	In-his-description
In-his-expression	In-his-usual
In-his-experience	In-seeming.

EXERCISE 22.

287. THE-BEAR AND-THE TWO TRAVELERS.—ÆSOP.

1. Two-men were traveling together when-they suddenly came upon-a bear. 2. One-of-them quickly hid in-the-branches of-a-tree; the other, seeing-that-he-would-be-taken, fell down, and-when-the-bear came up to-him, sought to feign-the appearance of-death as-much-as-possible. 3. The-bear soon-took his leave, for, it-is-said, he-will-only eat game that-has-been slain. 4. When-

THE S-SHUN AND INITIAL N HOOKS. 87

he-was-gone, the-other traveler came-down from-the tree, and jocularly said, "What-was-it that-the-bear spoke in-your ear?" 5. The-answer was, "He-gave-me this-advice: Never-travel with-one who-will-leave-you at-the approach of-danger." 6. Ill luck tries one's sincerity. (2 m).

288. The-physician in-his deposition says, that in-his-experience he-has-had-occasion many-times to-prescribe to-men-and-women of all nationalities. (4 times in 1 m).

289.   TRANSLATE.

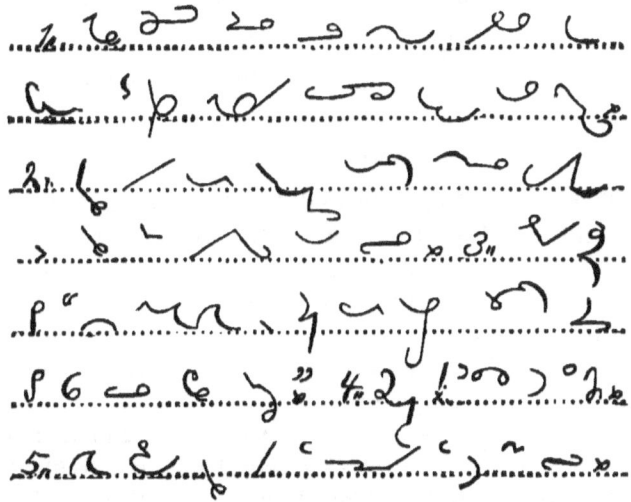

SELF-RELIANCE.—"There is no surer way to success in any undertaking than a firm reliance upon self. This applies with special force to the study of Short-hand. The most successful reporters we have ever known were those who did not depend upon the help of teacher or friend to learn Short-hand for them, but relied upon their own ability to succeed. *Real determination* will go as far, if not farther, than natural endowments; hence he who will rely upon the former may have as much, or even more, hope of success than one who is otherwise naturally fitted for the work, but lacks self-reliance."

LESSON XXIII.

290. **THE ST AND STR LOOPS.**

List stump disposed	gestation against justify
boaster stranger illustration	gesture manifest stage
stubborn statistics digestion	honestly spinster abstraction

THE ST-LOOP.

291. S is very often followed by *t*, forming the consonant double-sound *st*, of so frequent occurrence in our language, and which is expressed by an elongation of the s-circle, as in *list*, or *stump*. *Zd*, also, is sometimes denoted by this *loop*, as in *disposed*.

292. Like the s-circle, it may be followed by the s-shun hook, as in *gestation*; and implies *n* by being located on the n-hook side of straight letters, as in *against*.

293. Vocalize: Beast, boast, coast, feast, ghost, host, post, toast, taste, steal, waste, steed, twist; 1 pos. moist, steam, steep, accost. Without vowels: Placed, cast, chest, dust, fast, guest, haste, just, justify, list, against, arrest (ar), breakfast, detest, disgust, dishonest, distrust, earnest, enlist (el), gesture, harvest, indisposed, infest, intrust, invest, investigation, manifest, molest, must, most, pretext, stage, star (ar), state, statistics, stead, stole, stop, stomach, store, test, testify, text, trust, utmost, vast, west, stump, manifestation, almost, destiny, abreast, adjust, bequest, ——, blest, breast, bust, crest, dentist, digest, digestion, fantastic, fast, forest, frost, grist, incrust, inquest, jest, nest, protest, request, roast, rust, statesman, statute, stem, stern, stiff, sting, stitch, storm (ar), stubborn, stuff, stumble, vest, worst, wrist; 1 pos. August, cost, priest, least, still, stock, style, honest, honestly; 3 pos. last, past, stamp, attest.

THE STR-LOOP.

294. The st-loop, when written considerably broader, denotes the added r, as in *boaster*, or *stranger*.

295. Write: Cluster, lustre, master, illustration, monster, plaster, Sylvester, minister, spinster, register, obstruction, bluster, strange, stranger; 3 pos. administer, abstraction.

296. *Rem.* The st-loop should be made so slender as to appear like an elongated s-circle. It will then be readily distinguishable from the str-loop, which is written somewhat longer and considerably broader. The large loop, however, should not be rounded too much, or it will be liable to be confounded with the sez-circle.

297.   WORD AND PHRASE SIGNS.

To secure facile outlines, the circle only, instead of the loop, is often used when phrasing, as in *must-be* (ems-be).

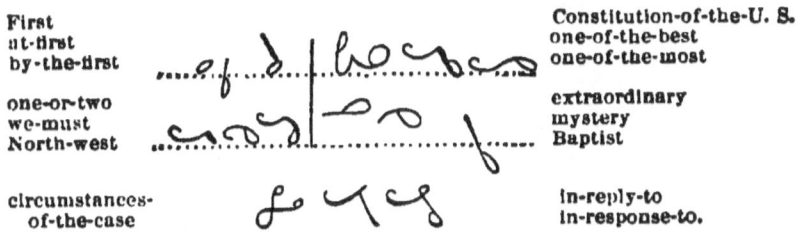

First
at-first
by-the-first

one-or-two
we-must
North-west

circumstances-
of-the-case

Constitution-of-the-U. S.
one-of-the-best
one-of-the-most

extraordinary
mystery
Baptist

in-reply-to
in-response-to.

EXERCISE 23.

298. 1. The-presence of-those whom we-love is-as-a-double life; absence, in-its-anxious longing and-sense-of vacancy, is-as-a-foretaste of-death. 2. We-that-live to please must please to-live. 3. It-is-best to-be with-those in-time that-we-hope to-be-with in-eternity. 4. They that govern must-make least noise. 5. Grace was in-all her steps, heaven in her eye. 6. By gaming we lose both our time-and-treasure, two things most precious to-the life of man. 7. Genius always gives-its-best at-first, prudence at-last. 8. Haste is-of-the devil. 9. Though I-am-always in-haste, I-am-never in-a-hurry. 10. Men love in-haste, but-they detest at-leisure. 11. Hope is-a lover's staff. 12. That-man lives twice, that-lives the-first life well. 13. The-grave is-a-common treasury to-which we-must-all be-taken. 14. Choose always **the-way-that** seems the-best, however rough it-may-be. (2 m 30 s).

299. 1. To step aside is human. 2. Music washes away from-the soul the-dust of-every day life. 3. Obstinacy is ever most-positive when-it-is-most in-the-wrong. 4. They-who forgive most shall-be-most forgiven. 5. Passion costs me too-much to bestow it upon every trifle. 6. To-climb steep hills requires slow pace at-first. 7. Every noble-work is-at-first impossible. 8. Time is generally the-best doctor. 9. In-poetry, which-is all-fable, truth is still the-perfection. 10. Poetry is truth dwelling in-beauty. 11. Ye stars, that are-the poetry of-heaven! 12. Praise is-only praise when-well addressed. 13. Solid padding against empty praise. 14. Live-this-day as-if-the-last. 15. Who-makes-the fairest show means-the-most deceit. 16. Small service, is true service while it-lasts. (2 m .

300. One-of-the-best and-most earnest of-the ministers in-the-North-west has-just-been advanced to-a higher post. (5 times in 1 m).

301. TRANSLATE.

NOTE.—"As a rule, the first thing to fail the scribe is his eye-sight. The position from which the least injury will result is that which admits the light upon the paper without either shining directly in the eyes or casting a reflection into them from the paper upon which one is writing."

LESSON XXIV.

THE LENGTHENED CURVE.

302.

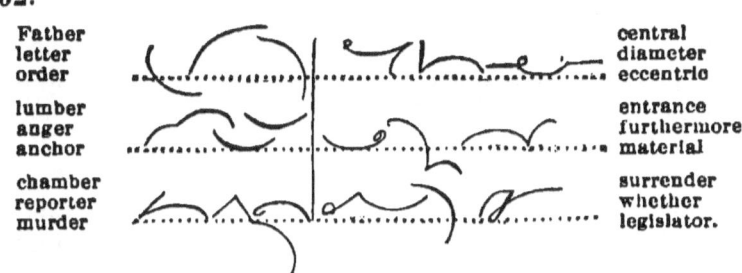

Father / letter / order — central / diameter / eccentric
lumber / anger / anchor — entrance / furthermore / material
chamber / reporter / murder — surrender / whether / legislator.

303. A curve written double its usual length signifies the addition of *thr*, as in *father*; sometimes, also, of *tr* or *dr*, as in *letter*, or *order*.

304. The tendency of the writer should be to make this more, rather than less, than double the standard length curve, in order that there may be no danger of confounding the two.

305. Write: Alexander, another, center, central, slender, diameter, eccentric, enter, entrance, father, further, furthermore, hinder, hindrance, material, maternal (nel), literal, mother, matter, order, render, calendar, senator, surrender, tender, thunder, thermometer, whether, wander, wonder, yonder; 1 pos. entire, entirely (el), immaterial, neither; 3 pos. neutral (el).

306. By lengthening *ing* and *emp*, the added *r*, *kr*, or *gr* is signified, as in *lumber*, *anger*, *anchor*.

307. Write: Anger, angry, amber, anchor, chamber, cumber, encumber, finger, hunger, linger, limber, murder, reporter (ar), slumber, temper.

EXERCISE 24.

308. THE THIEF AND HIS MOTHER.—ÆSOP.

1. A-boy steals a-lesson-book from-one of-his play-fellows and-takes-it home to-his-mother. 2. She-neglects to punish, and-

even encourages him. 3. He-next-time steals a-cloak and-brings-it to-her, when-she praises him still the-more. 4. The-youth soon-becomes-a-man, and-proceeds to steal things-of higher value. 5. He-is-taken while riding away on-a stolen horse, and-with shackles on, is-taken-away to-the place of public-execution. 6. His mother follows with-the-rest, and-strikes her-breast in sorrow; whereupon the-young-man says, 7. "I-wish-to say-something-to my-mother in-her ear." 8. She comes near him, when-he-quickly seizes her car with-his-teeth and-takes-it off. 9. His mother cries with-pain, but-the-son replies, "Ah mother, if-you-had-only beaten me when-I first stole that-lesson-book, I should-never-have come-to-this, nor would-the law oblige me now to ignominiously suffer the-punishment of-death." (2m 30s).

309. 1. Manners are stronger-than laws. 2. Order is heaven's first law. 3. He-that-will-be angry for-anything will-be angry for-nothing. 4. A-babe is-a-mother's anchor. 5. Whether your time calls you to-live or die, do both like-a prince. 6. He-conquers grief who-can-take-a firm-resolution. 7. It-matters-nothing how-a-man dies, but-how he-lives. 8. Love is, I-believe, an-entirely personal poem. 9 In-love anger is always false. (1m).

310. The-Judge calls-another reporter into-the chamber to-further the-taking of-testimony in-the-case of-the murder on-the Central-Railway. (4 times in 1 m).

311.   TRANSLATE.

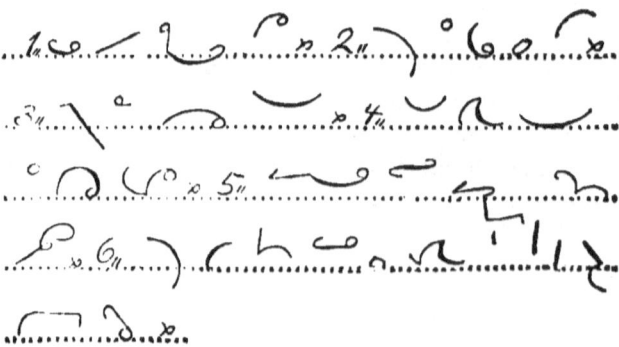

LESSON XXV.

THE HALVING PRINCIPLE.

312.

Bit
bed
cut
quote
bolt
slate
exert
start
merit
captive
circuit
educate
strict
transmit
reciprocate

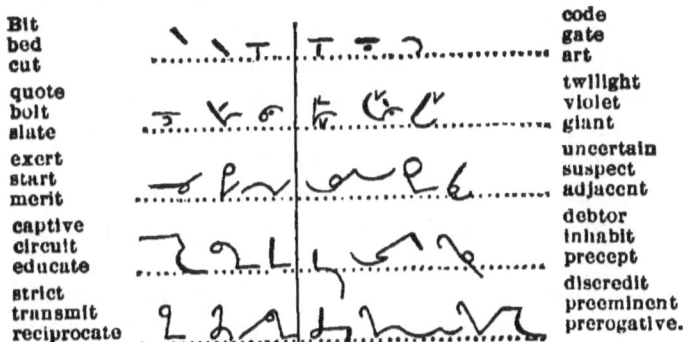

code
gate
art
twilight
violet
giant
uncertain
suspect
adjacent
debtor
inhabit
precept
discredit
preeminent
prerogative.

313. One of the most useful contrivances in the entire system, called the *Halving Principle*, is that by which a letter, when written half-length, indicates the addition of *t* or *d*. Thus, ＼ be, when written half its usual length, is read *be-te*, as in *bit*, or *be-de*, as in *bed* ;— kay, when halved, has the force of *kay-te*, as in *cut*, or *kay-de*, as in *code*. Te and de are the most frequently recurring consonants, and being cognates, no ambiguity results from the expression of both by one principle. Ray is halved only when combined with other consonants, as in *exert*, and written full length in such words as *rate*, and *right*.

314. In the following list, *t* is thus indicated: vocalize, boat, boot, coat, cut, gate, quote, cat, bolt, slate, mate, twilight, vault, violet, dolt, giant, nut, saint, gait, dote; 1 pos. cheat. Without vowels: Date, get, bet, debt, hate, art, late, net, let, met, fate, note, vote, sent, lift, left, sect, accent, enact, exact, exert, tact, adopt, better, insect, accept, acceptable, apostate, insert, suspect, little, result, smart, start, limit, merit, motive, docket, native, pocket, rabbit, recent, arithmetic, alphabet, instigate, assent, artifice, agent, intimate, repeat, remote, cadet, capital, locomotive, mathematics, ratify, petrify, rectify, rusticate, support, uncertain reject, auditor (ar), remit (ar), imitate, report, annotate, magnetic, resolute, resort, adjacent, adjudicate, adjunct, agitate, cognate, cottage, dogmatic, recapitulate, export, extinct, inject, intact, peasant, submit, musket, theft, upstart, captive, certain, circuit, debate, decent, deject, designate, desolate, detect, educate, debtor (ar), eject, elect (el), except, execute, habit, habitual, eminent, emulate, erect, estate, inhabit, innocent, irritate, legislate, originate, sentence, abject, Hamlet. (L-hook) implicate, pleasant, vegetable, duplicate, fluent; 1 pos. client, climate. (R-hook) intricate, precept, present, private, product, promote, prospect, protract, strict, subtract, tract, transmit, translate, attribute, bracelet, precinct, project, reciprocate, restrict, thrift, tribute, decrepit, affirmative, aggravate, appreciate, October, credit, deprecate, detract, discredit, extract, transcript, preeminent, prerogative, approximate.

315. CAUTION. Care should be taken that shortened letters are written *no more* than half their usual length, else the two will become confounded. The tendency should be to make them somewhat less than half the standard length.

316.   WORD AND PHRASE SIGNS.

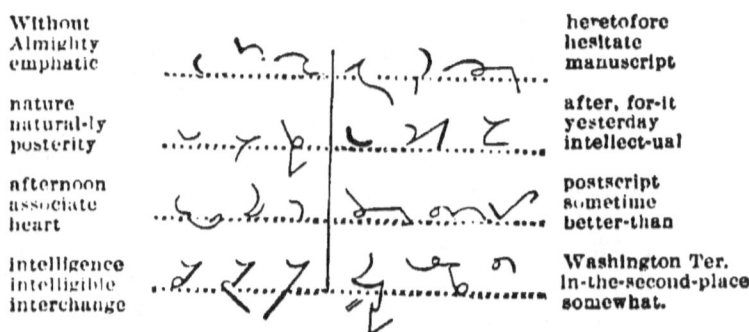

Without
Almighty
emphatic

nature
natural-ly
posterity

afternoon
associate
heart

intelligence
intelligible
interchange

heretofore
hesitate
manuscript

after, for-it
yesterday
intellect-ual

postscript
sometime
better-than

Washington Ter.
in-the-second-place
somewhat.

EXERCISE 25.

317. 1. Always rise from table with-an appetite, and-you-will-never sit down without-one. 2. When-we-feel a-strong desire to-thrust our advice upon others, it-is-usually because we suspect their weakness; but-we ought rather to suspect our-own. 3. To-be happy, we-must-be-true to nature, and-carry our age along-with us. 4. Beauty is-a-possession not our-own. 5. The-beautiful are-never desolate, but-some-one always loves-them. 6. It-is-better for-a young-man-to blush than to-turn pale. 7. Every Christian is born great because he-is-born for-heaven. 8. That-which-is-so universal as death must-be-a benefit. 9. We-speak of educating our children. Do-we-know that-our children also educate us? 10. Fortune is-the rod of-the-weak and-the staff of-the brave. 11. Let them obey who know how to-rule. 12. The-chains of habit are generally too-small to-be felt till they-are-too-strong to-be-broken. 13. Keep thy heart with-all diligence, for-out-of-it are-the issues of-life. (2 m 30 s).

318. We-will-certainly be-able very-soon to-make verbatim-reports of-the-eminent speakers in-the debate by-means-of-the stenographic art. (4 times in 1 m).

319. TRANSLATE.

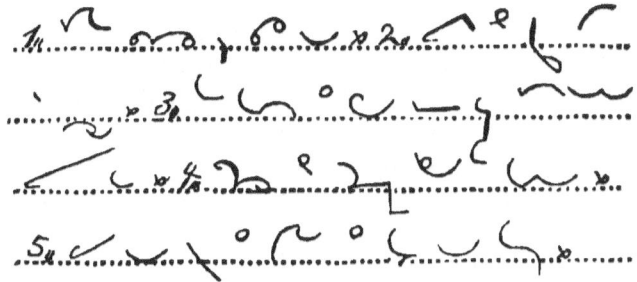

REMARK.—Shortened curves, in proportion to their length, are bent more than standard length letters. Care must be taken always to make a clear distinction between letters of different lengths. Not only must the halved letters *not be too long*, but those of standard length, also, should *not be too short*.

LESSON XXVI.

THE ADDED D.

320.

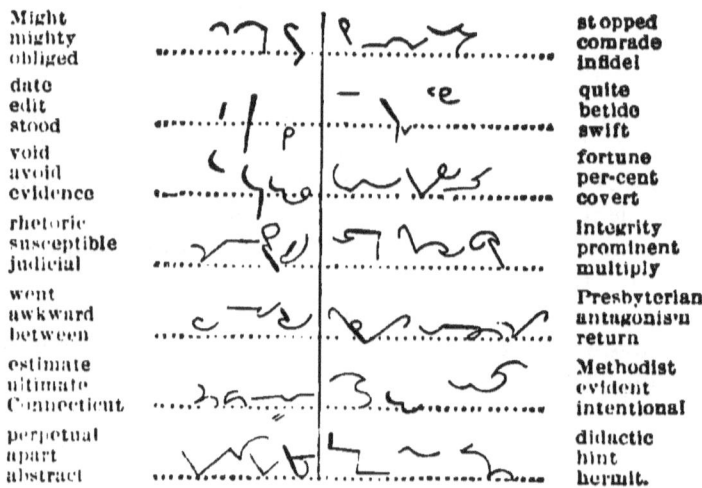

Might	stopped
mighty	comrade
obliged	infidel
date	quite
edit	betide
stood	swift
void	fortune
avoid	per-cent
evidence	covert
rhetoric	integrity
susceptible	prominent
judicial	multiply
went	Presbyterian
awkward	antagonism
between	return
estimate	Methodist
ultimate	evident
Connecticut	intentional
perpetual	didactic
apart	hint
abstract	hermit

321. Te or de, when followed by a final vowel, cannot be indicated by halving; e. g., *might* is expressed by the shortened em, while *mighty*, containing a final vowel, is written em-te.

322. Half-length consonants, when standing alone, are employed to denote words that contain but one vowel; e. g., halved de is used for *did*, while in *edit* the alphabetic de-te must be written. Halved ve, first position, denotes *void*, but in writing *avoid*, the full-length ve-de must be used. The application of this rule secures greater legibility, since the reader is expected to supply but one vowel when a shortened consonant stands alone.

323. In the following list, letters are shortened to express the sound *d*: Bed, could, good, shade, stood, decided, comrade, aided, instead, evidence, educated, invade, infidel.

324. Words composed entirely of horizontal and shortened letters, are written in the first position when the accented vowel is first-place.

325. Write: (1 pos.) caught, dot, east, bottom, quite, esteem, fight, deed, got, heat, did, light, bid, enlighten, God, meet, invite might, night, shot, slight, taught, indeed, speed, void, fit, knot, lightning, lot, soft, sort, spot; vocalize, feat, beat, naught, fought, betide, feed, knight, neat, salt, sheet, slide, spite, steed, swift, tide.

326. In the following list both t and d are expressed by halving: Accelerate, elucidate, fortune, per-cent, percentage, rhetoric, rapid, notify, dispute, active, actual, admit, apart, catalogue, decayed, didactic, covert, cupidity, melt, hint, assault, assimilate, athlete, dissect, dissent, dissipate, expedite, extort, exult, fanatic, hereditary, hermit, isolate, metaphor, oriental (el), ostentatious, perpetual, phonetic, refute, schedule (el), seldom, stupid; 1 pos. immature, despite, fault, appetite, exhort; 3 pos. act, adapt, addict, apt, doubt, foot, adequate, mutual, bad, adult, delude, adept, absent, fat, mute. (Sez-circle), necessitate, systematic, exasperate, susceptible, predecessor. (L-hook), article, beautiful, delicate, doubtful, emblematic, hospitable, judicial, notable. (R-hook), Godfrey, crabbed, crescent, proximate, Margaret, district, lubricate, dramatic, enervate, integral, promote, integrity, prejudice; 1 pos. prominent; 3 pos. attract, attractive, transact. (Rel-hook), paternal, promulgate, relent, multiply, federal, intolerable, multiplication. (W-hook), upward, acquaintance, went, warrant, quantity, wayward, reward, acquainted, Edward; 1 pos. wind, inward, awkward, wild, between, ward, wield; 3 pos. backward, outward. (F-hook), advocate, indefinite, defect, defective, photograph. (N-hook), pertinent, Presbyterian, manipulate, beneficent, patern, tenant, mandate, banquet, opponent, splendid, antagonism, benefit, return, candid, longitude; 1 pos. eastern. (Shun-hook), dedication, litigation, intention, intentional, estimation. (Loops), abstract, obstruct, distinct, distribute, investigate, stimulate, stipulate. (Initial n-hook), instruct.

327. The halving principle is applied in forming the past tense of regular verbs, as *obliged, stopped.*

328. Write: Packed, stopped, stocked, invested, molested, trusted, manifested, transcribed, obliged, displayed, employed, adopted, dispatched, solicited, specified, searched, risked, kept.

329. The principle is applied twice in each of the following words: Artist, captivate, capitulate, estimate, legitimate, illegitimate (el), mutilate, ultimate (el), fortunate, Connecticut, evident, protect, deduct, latitude, Methodist, rectitude, cataract; 1 pos. intent, mitigate; 3 pos. aptitude.

330. WORD AND PHRASE SIGNS.

1 Pos. feature, if-it, 2 after, for-it, 3 future, fact.

1 east, astonish-ed-ment, 2 establish-ed-ment.

1 it-ought, 3 at-it, it-would, it-had,

1 did, 2 do-it, 3 added, had-it.

1 of-it, 2 have-it, 3 have-had.

History — at-all-events
historian, eastern — east-and-west
Act-of-Congress — onward
wisdom — fear-of-God
Word-of-God — good-and-bad
People-of-God — in-the-world.

331. EXERCISE 26.

1. The-good is always beautiful, the-beautiful is good. 2. Goodness is beauty in-its-best estate. 3. Men often make-up in wrath what they-want in reason. 4. Let-not the-sun go-down upon thy wrath. 5. All things are artificial, for nature is-the-art of-God. 6. Biography is-the home aspect of history. 7. The-desire of knowledge, like thirst of-riches, increases ever with-the acquisition of-it. 8. Life is like wine; he-who-would drink it pure must drain it to-the dregs. 9. Literature is-the-thought of-thinking souls. 10. Doing-good is-the-only certainly happy action of-a-man's life. 11. A-life that-is-worth living at-all is worth writing minutely. 12. The-universe would-not-be rich enough to buy the-vote of-an honest man. 13. Character is-a-perfectly educated

will. 14. It-were joy to die if-there-be gods, and-sad to-live if-there-be none. 15. It-is-better to-desire than-to enjoy; to-love than-to-be-loved. 16. If-you-do what-you should-not, you-must-bear what-you would-not. 17. If-there-was-no future-life our-souls would-not thirst for-it. 18. No-one can-be-said to-be until he-is dead. 19. I-like a-good hater. (3 m).

332. True wisdom is-to know what-is-best worth knowing, and-to-do what-is-best worth doing. (6 times in 1 m).

333. TRANSLATE.

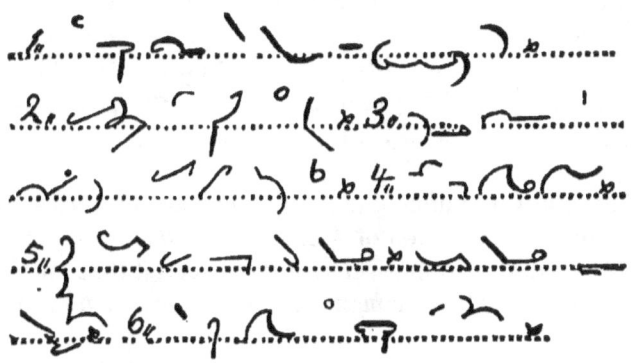

NOTE.—"Use the best quality of writing fluid. There is about as much difference between the various kinds of ink that are generally kept for sale as there is between a charcoal pencil and a good gold pen. And what is worse, very few people have any idea that there is any difference in ink. Any liquid that will make a colored mark, even though it be indigo water, is to the majority of people equally as good as the best writing fluid. Good ink is just as essential as good pens and paper. Ink that flows freely from the pen should be used. The stand or bottle should be kept securely corked while not in use, so as to prevent the ink from becoming thick by evaporation or from dust settling in it."

LESSON XXVII.

334. SHORTENED DOUBLE CONSONANTS.

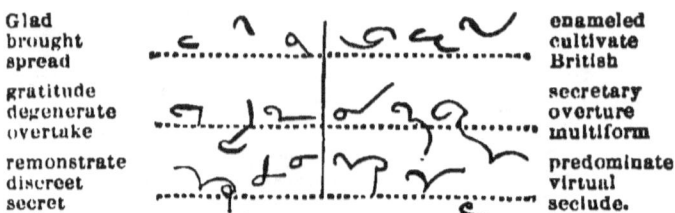

Glad, brought, spread, gratitude, degenerate, overtake, remonstrate, discreet, secret, enameled, cultivate, British, secretary, overture, multiform, predominate, virtual, seclude.

335. Letters of the double and triple consonant series, are also halved to signify the addition of *t* or *d*, as in *glad, brought, spread, enameled*. In these examples, it will be observed that both sounds expressed by the double consonant are pronounced *before* the added t or d.

336. Using the l-hook and vowels: Plate, blade, plat; 1 pos. fleet, flight, bleed, clod, deplete; (without vowels), exclude, inflate, blood, glad, flood, cultivate, cultivation, explode, include, preclude, replied, tumbled, coupled, displayed, tangled, entitled, employed; smuggled, doubled, assembled, rambled, pamphlet, multiform; 1 pos. plead, blot, glide, plot; 3 pos. cloud, seclude. (R-hook) vocalize, trait, brute, prayed, crowed, cried, migrate; 1 pos. creed, trite; (without vowels), destroyed, gathered, labored, prospered, papered, uttered, shirt, tempered, altered, betrayed, muttered, offered, silvered, measured, treasured, chartered, recurred, scattered, suffered, illustrated, clamored, flattered, traveled, troubled, fluttered, glittered, hammered, scrupled, arbitrate, aristocrat, British, culprit, gratitude, degenerate, fertile, frustrate, penetrate, perpetrate, pervert, shrewd, vibrate, virtual, virtuous, great, retreat, regret, grade, grateful, celebrate, democrat, credible, degrade, defraud, hatred, effort, emigrate, third, trade, hypocrite, gratify, vertical, bread, overtake, predicate, cupboard, verdict, thread, dread, intrude, tread, sacred, spread, straight, secretary, demonstrate, Elbert, Frederick, Richard, Robert, Gertrude, Albert, Alfred;

SHORTENED DOUBLE CONSONANTS.

(using ar), overture, orchard, remonstrate; 1 pos. discreet, entreat, fright, greet, treat, trot, predominate, prominent, bright, brought, fraught, freedom, pride, immigrate, street, secret; 3 pos. crowd, crude, fruit, proud, graduate, scrutiny.

337.   WORD AND PHRASE SIGNS.

 1 Pos. particular-ly, 2 opportunity, 3 part-y.

 1 according-ly, creature, 2 cared, occurred, 3 cured.

 1 till-it, 2 tell-it, 3 until-it.

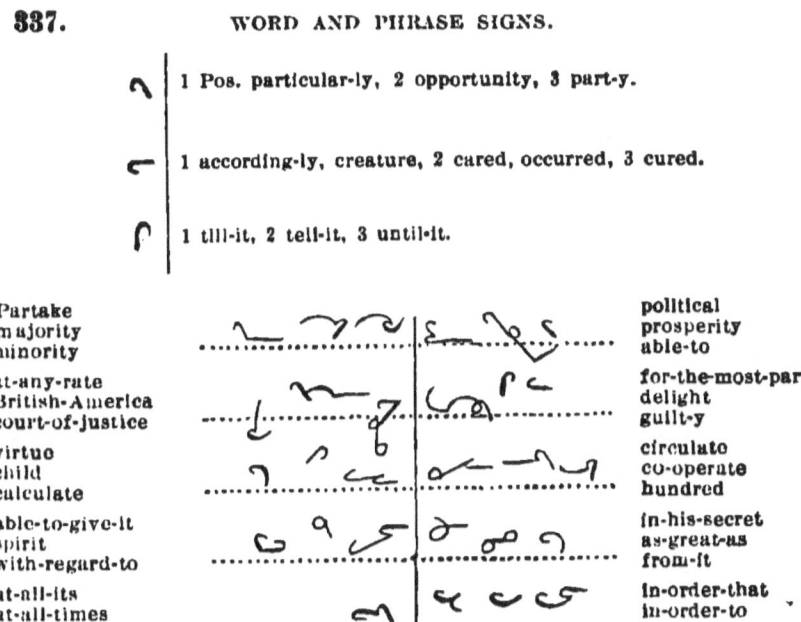

Partake
majority
minority

at-any-rate
British-America
court-of-justice

virtue
child
calculate

able-to-give-it
spirit
with-regard-to

at-all-its
at-all-times
Great-Britain

political
prosperity
able-to

for-the-most-part
delight
guilt-y

circulate
co-operate
hundred

in-his-secret
as-great-as
from-it

in-order-that
in-order-to
in-regard-to.

EXERCISE 27.

338. 1. To-do-an evil action is base; to-do a-good action, without incurring danger, is common enough; but it-is-the-part of-a good-man to-do great-and noble deeds, though-he risks everything. 2. Angels are bright still, though-the brightest fell. 3. Men resemble the-gods in-nothing so-much-as in-doing-good to-their fellow-creatures. 4. Many delight more in-giving of-presents than in-paying debts. 5. Heaven from all-creatures hides the-book of fate. 6. A-good heart will, at-all-times, betray the-best head in-the-world. 7. The-greatest trust between man-and-man is-the-trust of-giving-counsel. 8. The-next dreadful thing to-a battle lost is-a battle won. 9. It-is seldom the-case that beautiful persons are otherwise of-great-virtue. 10. A-book may-be as-great-a thing as-a battle. 11. When clouds are-seen wise-men put on-their cloaks. 12. There-can-be no Christianity where-there-is-no charity. 13. What-can-the Creator see with greater pleasure than-a-happy creature? 14. The-last enemy that-shall-be destroyed is death. 15. The-better part of valor is discretion. 16. He-is-not-only idle who-does-nothing, but-he-is idle who-might-be better employed. 17. To know how to-wait is-the-great secret of-success. (3 m).

339. You-should-cultivate a-good-memory in-order-that, at-all-times, you-may-be-able-to-report the-exact-evidence which, in-courts-of-justice, is sometimes given at-the rate of two hundred a-minute. (3 times in 1 m).

340. TRANSLATE.

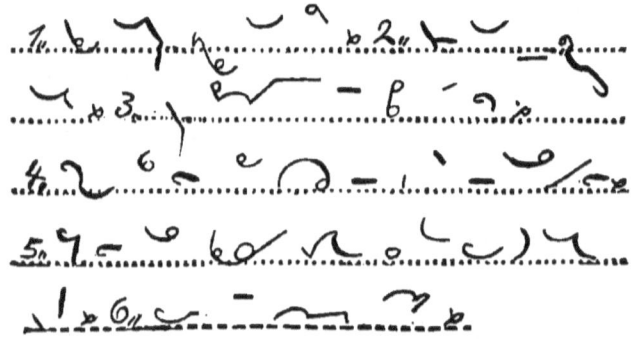

NOTE.—" Hold your paper or note-book firmly with the left hand. This can best be done by placing the tips of the fingers of the left hand upon the edge of the paper at right-angles with the right hand, keeping the thumb against the edge of the paper. By a slight pressure of the fingers the paper can be held firmly in place while, with the thumb at the edge of the paper, the page can be readily turned with it as soon as the last line is written. This is a far more important suggestion than it may seem, since but poor work, at best, can be done unless the paper is firmly held in its place.

LESSON XXVIII.

SHORTENED FINAL-HOOK CONSONANTS.

341.

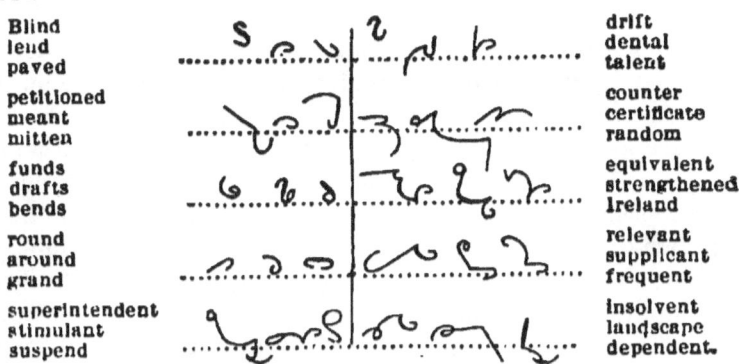

Blind	drift
lend	dental
paved	talent
petitioned	counter
meant	certificate
mitten	random
funds	equivalent
drafts	strengthened
bends	Ireland
round	relevant
around	supplicant
grand	frequent
superintendent	insolvent
stimulant	landscape
suspend	dependent.

342. Consonants to which a final hook is joined are also halved, both stem and hook being pronounced before the added t or d, as in *blind, lend, paved, petitioned*. *Meant*, for instance, is expressed by the halved ⌒ *men*, which is equivalent to men-te. Here the character *men* is regarded as indivisible, and is pronounced first, it not being allowable in such case to sound *t* immediately after em, as in *met*, before the reading of *n*, expressed by the final hook. Hence, in *mitten*, and similar words, in which *t* occurs before the final hook, the halving principle cannot be applied.

343. But the s-circle is invariably read after t or d, as in *funds, drafts, bends*.

344. Write, using the f-hook: Craft; 1 pos. gift, drift. (N-hook), count, tent, faint, fund, lent, mend, paint, vent, dent, dental, tend, rent, lend, bound, bend, round, spend, stand, surround, silent, repent, amend, extent, fount, fountain, indent, mound, refund, talent, vacant, violent, moment, accident, disappoint, disband, husband, candor (ar), certificate, certify, event, ancient, potent, infant, lament, phantom, mount, mountain, patent, patient, payment, country, ardent, enchant, demand, random, extend, mankind, tendency, depend, exorbitant, expedient, valient, resident, serpent, servant, argument, Atlantic, excellent, equivalent, basement, attentive, strengthened, coincident, detriment, urgent, cement, encounter, discount, impotent, delinquent, distant, document, cogent, instant, elephant, enactment, repugnant, impediment, identity, opulent, incident, stimulant, suspend, amazement, announcement, romantic, solvent, subsequent, observant, abscond, memorandum, Maryland, Richmond, Edmund, Omnipotent; (using el), elegant, element, gentle, aliment, boundless, incidental, fundamental, bundle, candle; (using ar), arrogant, indenture, counter, surmount, venture, remnant, around, remainder, slander, Ireland, Raymond, Roland; 1 pos. bond, fond, augment, authentic, joined, occupant, joint, point, bind, find, kind, appoint, diamond; 3 pos. amusement, apparent, rudiment, expand, land, landscape, pound, band, cant. (N and l hooks), plant, blunt, applicant, supplicant, blend, gland, plunder (ar), blunder (ar), Clement; 1 pos. blind; 3 pos. bland. (N and r hooks), grand, brand, frantic, front, vagrant, grand-jury, president, encouragement, frequent, predicament, precedent, prevent, reprimand, superintend, transparent, flagrant, profound, divergent, fragrant, pretend, fragment, brilliant, ingredient; 1 pos. grind, immigrant, print; 3 pos. ground. (N and f hooks), pavement, extravagant, covenant, achievment, advancement (des-ment), reverend. (N-hook twice), countenance, tangent, penitent, liniment, monument, mendicant, abundant, ornament. (Initial n-hook), insolent, insolvent. (Principle applied twice , respondent, redundant, despondent candidate, resentment, sentiment, amendment, vindicate; 1 pos. treatment, appointment, predominant.

NOTE.—"There are two good reasons why it pays to write a small hand. I do not mean by this a cramped style, which is as difficult to write and looks no better than the other extreme, a large or sprawling style. It takes a great deal more time to write a character twice as long as need be than it does to strike it the proper length. To save time is the one thing for which Short-hand is learned, and to spread the characters out over double the necessary amount of paper, is but to defeat, in a great measure, the end for which it is being used."

SHORTENED FINAL-HOOK CONSONANTS. 105

845. WORD AND PHRASE SIGNS.

1 Pos. gentlemen, 2 gentleman, 3 imagined.

1 cannot, kind, 2 can-it, 3 account.

1 mind, 2 may-not, 3 movement, mount.

1 behind, be-not, 3 bound.

1 which-ought-not, 2 which-not, 3 which-would-not, which-had-not.

1 which-ought-to-have-had, 2 which-have-had, 3 which-would-have-had.

1 it-ought-not, 2 it-not, 3 it-would-not, it-had-not.

1 did-not, 2 do-not, 3 had-not.

1 it-ought-to-have-had, 3 it-would-have-had.

1 such-ought-to-have-had, 2 such-have-had, 3 such-would-have-had.

2 such-are-not, 3 such-were-not.

1 on-either-hand, 2 they-are-not, on-the-other-hand.

1 is-it, 2 as-it, 3 use-it.

Derivative
infinite
profit, prophet
temperament
testament
will-not
which-are-not
which-were-not
dare-not
appoint
upon-it
on-the-one-hand

intelligent
island
record
it-will-not
which-will-not
great-extent
give-it
gave-it
it-will-have-had
we-are-not
have-not
in-point-of-fact.

346. **EXERCISE 28.**

1. Idlers cannot-find time to-be idle, or-the-industrious to-be at-leisure. 2. We-must-always-be doing, or suffering. 3. How slow the-time to-the warm soul, that, in-the-very instant it forms, would-execute a-great design! 4. The-least movement is-of-importance to all nature. 5. The-entire ocean is affected by-a pebble. 6. Nature has inclined us to-love-men. 7. The-world cannot-do-without great-men, but-great-men are troublesome to-the-world. 8. In-life we-shall-find many-men that-are-great, and-some-men that-are-good, but-very few-men that-are-both great-and-good. 9. A-man is sure to-dream enough before-he dies, without-making arrangements for-the-purpose. 10. I-do-not give, but-lend myself to business. 11. Good counsels observed are-claims to-grace. 12. If-there-is-anything that keeps the-mind open-to angel visits, and-repels the-ministry of ill, it-is human-love. 13. Age, that-lessens the-enjoyment of-life, increases our desire of-living. 14. We-do-not count a-man's years until he-has-nothing-else to-count. 15. I-have-always observed that to-succeed in-the-world we-must-be foolish in appearance, but in-reality wise. 16. Beauty lives with kindness. 17. You-do-not believe, you only believe that-you-believe. 18. Next to acquiring good-friends, the-best acquisition is-that-of-good-books. 19. I-can promise to-be candid, but I-cannot promise to-be impartial. 20. There-is-no-such-thing as chance; and-what seems to us merest accident springs from-the-deepest source of-destiny. 21. I-have often thought of-death, and-I-find it the-least of all evils. 22. The-greatest difficulties lie where-we-are-not looking for-them. 23. How disappointment tracks-the steps of hope! 24. Do-not-ask if a-man has-been through college; ask if-a-college has-been through-him, if-he-is-a walking university. 25. Genius does what-it-must, and-talent does what-it-can. 26. There-is-in-man a-higher aim than love of happiness; he-can-do without happiness, and-instead thereof find blessedness. (4 m 30 s).

347. The-greatest events of-an-age are-its-best thoughts. It-is-the nature of-thought to-find its-way into-action. (5 time.' in 1 m).

SHORTENED LIQUIDS.

348. TRANSLATE.

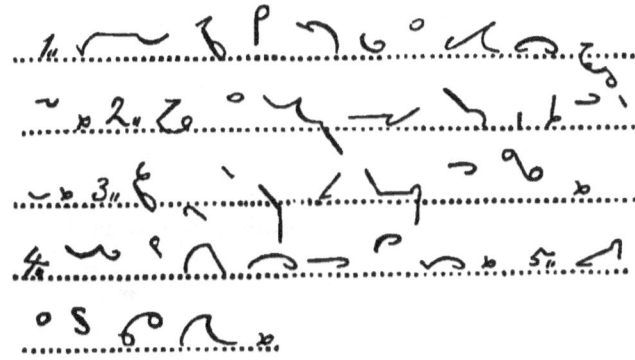

LESSON XXIX.

SHORTENED LIQUIDS.

349.

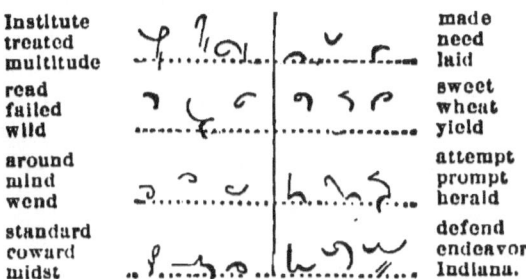

Institute			made
treated			need
multitude			laid
read			sweet
failed			wheat
wild			yield
around			attempt
mind			prompt
wend			herald
standard			defend
coward			endeavor
midst			Indiana.

350. It is often inexpedient to use a half-length letter when the angle formed by its juncture with another consonant is not sufficient to render it readily distinguishable: e. g., in *looked*, the shortened kay should not be used, since the combination lay-ket, when written quickly, would have the appearance of lengthened lay. For similar reasons the halved ish should not be used after lay; en, ef, or ve after te or de; te after te or de; or kay after ef or ve.

351. A final half-length to denoting *tute*, *tude*, or *ted*, is disjoined in some cases in order to render it distinguishable, as in *institute*, *treated*, *multitude*.

352. ⌒ El, ⌐ ar, ⌒ em, and ⌣ en, are thickened when halved to express *d*, as in *made*, *need*, *laid*, *read*. This practice adds to the legibility of short-hand, and gives rise to no ambiguity, since ⌒ yea, ⌐ way, ⌒ emp, and ⌣ ing are not shortened. Only the downward *l* is used when thickened to express the added *d*, as in *failed*. These letters, however, are not shaded when either the w or n hook is attached, as in *wild*, *around*, *mind*, *wend*.

353. Exceptions. In a very few cases way, yea, and emp′, are halved, as in *sweet*, *wheat*, *yield*, *attempt*, *prompt*.

354. Using *ld*, write: Load, scold, lead, fold, manifold, mould, Springfield, unfold, old, laid, sold, herald, crawled, drilled; 1 pos. lead, leader, mild, field; 3 pos. loud, mood; (rd), absurd, afford, standard, deplored, beard, yard, Leonard, sword, coward; 1 pos. kindred, ordinance, read, redeem, redemption; (md), made, mud, amidst, modify, meditate, blamed, inflamed, claimed, blossomed, drummed, toiled, meddle; 1 pos. medium, modulation, mid, midnight, middle, midst, model, modern, moderate; 3 pos. mad; (nd), defend, end, endless (el), send, defendant, ascend, ascendant, descend, descendant, index, indebted, endeavor. indolence (el), indolent, indigent, indivisible, indulge (el), reasoned. Independent, errand, transcend; 1 pos. need, needless (el), needle (el). Indian, Indiana, indicate, indication, intend; 3 pos. sand. (Disjoined ted), dated, destitute, institute, dreaded; 3 pos. attitude.

355. WORD AND PHRASE SIGNS.

⌒ 1 Pos. immediate-ly, 2 made, 3 **mad.**

⌣ 1 need, 2 end, under, 3 **hand.**

⌒ 1 lead, 2 hold, held, old, load, 3 **loud.**

↘ 1 Lord, read, 2 heard, word, 3 **hard.**

SHORTENED LIQUIDS. 109

World
handsome
hardware
downward
forward
individual
short-hand
undergo
hand-in-hand

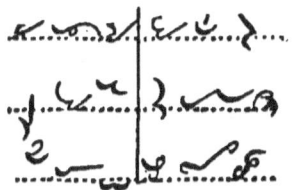

afterward
beforehand
behold, beheld
hazard
hand-writing
landlord
understand
greater-than
ladies-and-gentlemen.

356. EXERCISE 29.

1. Adversity is-the-trial of-principle. 2. Without-it, a-man hardly knows whether he-is-honest or-not. 3. By steps we-may ascend to God. 4. Act well at-the moment, and-you-have performed a-good action to all-eternity. 5. For-my-own part, I-had-rather-be old only-a-short-time than-be old before I-really am so. 6. As-we grow old we-become more foolish and-more wise. 7. Every-man desires to-live-long, but no-man would-be-old. 8. The-path of-glory leads but-to-the grave. 9. A-merry heart doeth good like-a-medicine, but-a-broken spirit drieth the-bones. 10. Heaven's eternal wisdom has decreed that man of man should-ever-stand in-need. 11. He-makes no friend who-never had-a foe. 12. Hatred is nearly always honest, rarely if-ever assumed. 13. So-much cannot-be-said for-love. 14. In a-better-world we-will-find our young years and-our old friends. 15. They-say women and-music should-never-be dated. 16. Few people know how to-be-old. 17. O, how-much more doth beauty beauteous seem by-that sweet ornament which truth doth give! 18. There's-a divinity that-shapes our ends, rough hew them how we-will. 19. Genius makes-its observations in-short-hand; talent writes-them-out at-length. 20. The-miserable have-no-other medicine, but-only hope. 21. Where-there-is-no hope there-can-be no endeavor. (3 m).

357. The-great-man is-he who, in-the-midst of-the crowd keeps with-perfect sweetness the-independence of solitude. (5 times in 1 m).

858. TRANSLATE.

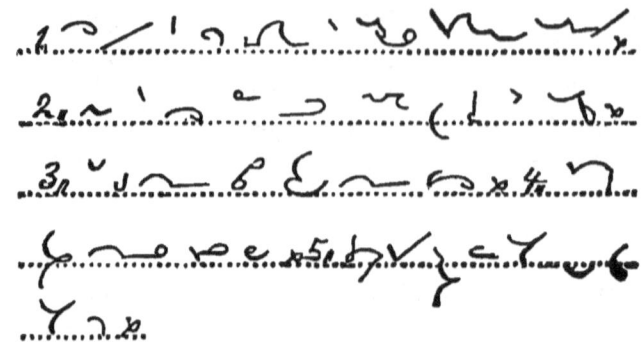

LESSON XXX.

INTERVOCALIZATION.

359.

Core		gill
gall		moral
margrave		shoal
knoll		chart
cheer		chill
sport		accord
cork		insurance
epicure		lecture
jealous		secure
prevail		require
qualify		school
legislature		corporal
derogatory		North-Carolina
persevere		California
tolerable		Delaware
mortal		Baltimore
ordinary		correspondent
volunteer-ary		preliminary.

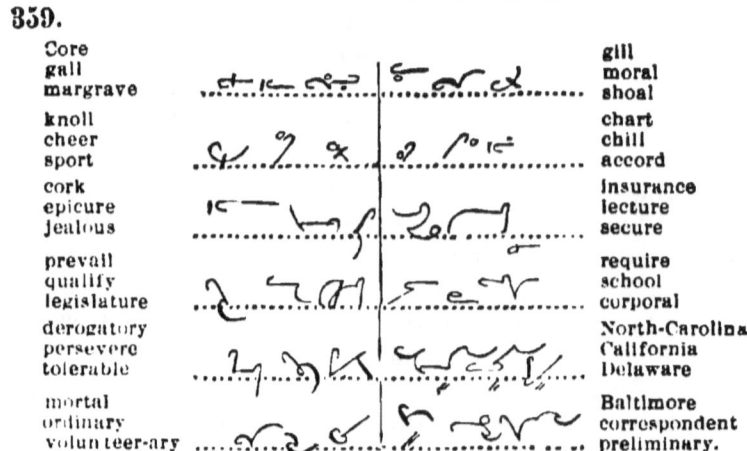

360. Any letter of the double or triple consonant series may be *intervocalized,* by which is meant the vowel may be placed in such a manner as to be read between the two consonants. E. g., ker, with the dash vowel–*o* struck through it, is read *core*. Here the vowel, by being written in this manner, is read after kay and before ar. Second and third place dash vowels are struck through

INTERVOCALIZATION. 111

the stems, but first-place dashes are written just before them, as in *gall*. When a dot-vowel is to be written, a small circle is used, and placed before the stem if long, as in *Margrave*, and after it if short, as in *gill*.

361. This principle is rarely applied in actual reporting, but a considerable advantage is nevertheless secured by it; for, since it is a rule to form no outline too brief for vocalization, the stems *per, ber, ter, der*, etc., would have to be written out in quite a number of words in which double consonants may now be used instead. In *moral*, for example, the outline mer-lay is proper, since it will admit of vocalization; otherwise, the r-hook could not be employed.

362. Write: Fur, cur, core, cull, gull, gall, gill, gal, shoal, knoll, cheer, sport, fort, margrave, board, port, carve, chart, chill, dirt, nurse, purse, spur, terse, encore, epicure; 1 pos. accord, cork; (without vowels), course, college, derange, elaborate, enormity, demoralize, impulse, infer infirm, jealous, journey, insurance, invalid, lecture, curb, nerve, nervous, North, moral, morality, nourish, perceive, perjure, person, shirk, engineer, picture, pilgrim, preliminary, prevail, pursue, pursued, corner, shoulder, qualify, legislature, recall, regulate, require, ridicule, darling, school, sharp, thirst, signature, telegram, till, term, Thursday, treasure, utility, volume, voluminous, vulgar, abjure, agriculture, armful, balcony, barter, capture, cargo, collateral, corporal, corporate, incorporate, corroborate, courteous, culture, decorum, derogatory, calico, director, disparage, partial, impartial, distil, divulge, falter, farthing, garnish, invulnerable, marble, marshal, miracle, nursery, nurture, obscure, parcel, parlor, persevere, porter, portray, purple, shark, singular, tolerable, torpedo, turkey, valid, valedictory, vinegar, volcano, assurance, Charles, George, Jerome, Philip, Martha, Georgia, New-Jersey, North-Carolina, Virginia, Columbia; 1 pos. column, skill, cord, discord, gild, guilt; 3 pos. assure, secure, security. (Sez), persist, paralysis, parenthesis. (W-hook), Delaware. (F-hook), gulf, turf, telegraph, adventure, imperative, California, narrative. (N-hook), burden, margin, pardon, pertain, diligence, jurisprudence, performance, terminate, German, bargain, cosmopolitan, culminate, galvanic, Mormon, northeastern, parlance, Calvin, Martin, Morgan,

Caroline. (Shun-hook), perception, circulation, admiration, partition, jurisdiction, corruption, regulation. (Rel-hook), journal, normal, personal, carnal, phrenology. (Halving), carpenter, garment, delegate, departure (ar), invert, dilapidate, impart, market, merchant, merchandise, mercantile (el), mortal, ordinary, particle, partner, pursuant, regard, record, transport, voluntary, volunteer, Vermont, Baltimore, Pittsburg, deliberate, correspond, correspondence, correspondent, default, dormant, escort, forbid, parliament, persecute, portrait, purport, recorder, scaffold, scarlet, target, jurist, told, velvet, palpitate, Archibald, Arnold, Baldwin, Gilbert, Herbert (ar).

363.   EXERCISE 30.

1. Action is eloquence, and-the eyes of-the ignorant more learned than their ears. 2. It-is-often better to-have-a-great-deal of harm happen to-one than-a-little; a-great-deal may arouse you to-remove what-a-little will-only accustom-you to endure. 3. There-is-nothing that-makes-its-way more directly to-the soul than beauty. 4. We-make way for-the-man who boldly pushes past us. 5. Your little child is-your-only true democrat. 6. Childhood shows-the-man, as-the morning shows-the-day. 7. The-child is father of-the man. 8. Defeat is-a-school in-which truth always grows strong. 9. Admiration is-the daughter of-ignorance. (1 m 30 s).

364. Rich-men without wisdom-and learning are-called sheep with golden fleeces. (9 times in 1 m).

365.   TRANSLATE.

LESSON XXXI.

366. PREFIXES

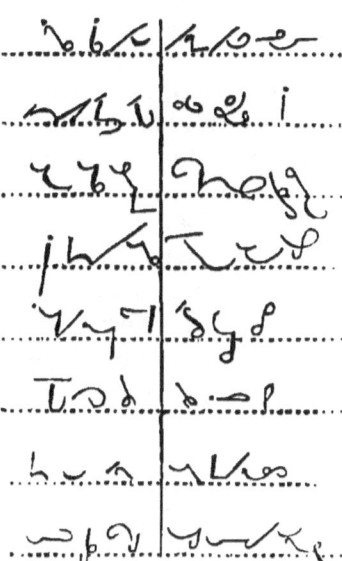

Compress	reconstruct
couduce	recognition
recommend	excommunicate
countermarch	circumvent
contradiction	self-consciousness
contribution	commit
interview	maladministration
introduce	postpone
antiseptic	supervene
commodity	accompany
contemporary	internal
interpose	inconsistent
commentary	counterbalance
community	confidence
credulity	circumstance
accommodation	composition
commission	conquest
compensation	constitute
contempt	interrupt
command	conductor
counterpart	commencement
interrogation	incompetent
discontent	antiquary
malcontent	incomprehensible.

367. The commonest *Prefixes* and *Affixes* are provided with brief signs, most of which are joined to the main outline. *Com* and *con* are indicated by a dot, as in *compress* or *conduce*. In most cases, however, this dot is entirely omitted with no loss of legibility. *Com, con,* and *cog,* when medial, are expressed by disjoining the preceding from the following portion of the word, as in *recommend, reconstruct, recognition.* *Counter, contra-i-o,* are indicated by a slanting tick, as in *countermarch, contradiction, contribution.* *Circum,* and *self,* are denoted by the *s-circle,* as in *circumvent, self-consciousness.* *Inter, intro,* and *anti,* are indicated by the shortened en, joined to the remaining part of the word, as in *interview, introduce, antiseptic.* *Mal, post,* and *super,* are commonly expressed by the characters *mel, pes,* and *spr,* as in *maladministration, postpone, supervene.*

368. In the following list, the prefixes printed in italics are to be represented by the signs just explained. The syllables enclosed in brackets need not be written.

REPORTING STYLE OF SHORT-HAND.

Com*m*it, com*m*odity, com*p*ass, com*p*ensate, compose, convict, [con]tinual (cl), [con]temporary (cmp), *inter*pose, console, *inter*fere, *accom*pany, *circum*navigate, conceit, conciliate, *intro*duce, concise, *inter*est, condemn, confess, *counter*march, decompose, discompose, dis[con]tinue, *inter*nal, in[con]sistent, recognize, reconcile, *self*ish, un[con]scious, *anti*thesis, commentary, committee, compile, concede, *counter*check, *post*paid, conspicuous, conspire, [con]veyance, convoke, *mis*conceive, [com]pare, [com]pany, [com]parison, conceive, [con]form, [con]scientious, [con]scious, [con]sist; 1 pos. consign, conceal, *counter*sign; 3 pos. conduce, community, [con]sume, *inter*view. (L-hook), constable, *incom*parable, *inconceiva*ble, [accom]plish, conjugal, convulse, [com]pel, [con]flict, *inter*val. (R-hook), concur, confer, *circum*ference, *circum*scribe, *incom*prehensible, *pre*conceive, *self*-control, compress, [con]firm, [con]gress, [con]spiracy, [con]trary, [con]troversy, [con]verse, *enter*prise; 1 pos. [com]prise, [com]promise; 3 pos. [con]struc, *mis*construc. (W-hook), *anti*quary, *counter*work. (F-hook), concave, [con]servative, [con]trive, [con]trivance. (N-hook), concurrence, [con]tain, [con]tains, *contine*, *counter*balance, *contra*vene, in[con]venience, re[com]pense, *com*pendium, condolence, [con]fidence, congenial, [circum]stance, [com]panion, [com]plain, [con]cern, [con]science, [con]stancy, [con]strain, [con]venience, [con]vince, [con]tinuance, *enter*tain, *inter*line, *inter*vene; 1 pos. *counter*mine. (Shun-hook), *accom*modation, *circum*locution, [com]mission, [com]petition, *com*pulsion, [con]fession, *counter*action, *recogni*tion, *recomm*endation, [con]sideration, *antic*ipation, [com]plexion, [con]cession, [con]clusion, [com]descension, [con]demnation, [con]jugation, *conse*cration, [con]solidation, [con]viction, [con]templation (emp), *inter*pretation, *con*vulsion, [com]bination, [con]dition, [con]ception, *inter*diction, *contri*bution, *con*version, *inter*jection, un[con]ditional, [com]gregation; 1 pos. [com]pletion; 3 pos. confusion, [com]passion. (S-shun-hook), [com]pensation, [com]position. (St-loop), *conquest*, *contest*, contrast, *contra*distinction, *com*posed, *conge*stion, *context*, [con]stitute, [con]stitution. (Halving), *accom*modate, *circum*spect, *com*bat, [con]template (emp), [con]tempt, [comm]and, [com]ment, [con]duct, *com*pute, [con]sent, *con*cert, [con]descend, *con*fiscate, [con]sult, *counter*part, *inter*dict, dis[con]nect, *com*patible, *incom*patible, *incom*plete, *inter*sect,

PREFIXES.   115

mis[con]duct, *recommend*, *inter*rupt, *self*-esteem, *anti*cipate, *anti*dote, [comm]andment,. [con]duct, [con]ductor, *non*conductor, *ex*communicate, [comm]encement, *rec*onstruct, [com]parative, [com]plicate, [com]pliment, [con]solidate, [con]sonant, [con]struct, [con]tact, [con]tribute, [contra]dict; 1 pos. *con*fide, *con*sort, *counter*feit, *complete*, [con]venient, *inter*rogate, *inter*rogation; 3 pos. [con]clude, [comm]unicate. (R-hook), [com]fort, concurred, *con*cordance, *con*vert, [con]gratulate, [con]gratulation, *inter*pret; 1 pos. *con*crete. (N-hook), *com*pound, [con]tingent, dis-[con]tent, *mal*content, [con]tent, [con]straint, incompetent (content), [com]plained, [con]fident, [con]sistent, [con]stant, [con]stantly (el), [con]tent, in[con]sistent; 3 pos. *con*found.

369.   WORD-SIGNS.

Construction
confidential
conjunction
consequence
consequent
consequential

unconcern
comprehend
antiquity
consider
consideration
reconsider.

EXERCISE 31.

370. 1. Our-actions are our-own; their consequences belong to-heaven. 2. No-man should-be so-much taken-up in-the-search of-truth, as thereby to neglect the-more-necessary duties of-active-life; for after-all is-done, it-is-action only that gives a-true value and-commendation to-virtue. 3. Active natures are rarely melancholy. 4. Words are-good, but-there-is-something-better. 5. The-best is-not-to-be explained by-words. 6. The-spirit in-which-we act is-the-chief matter. 7. Action can only-be understood and-represented by-the-spirit. 8. No-one knows what he-is-doing while he-is acting rightly, but of-what-is wrong we-are-always conscious. 9. Prosperity is too apt to-prevent us from-examining our conduct, but as adversity leads us to-think properly of-our state, it-is-most beneficial to us. 10. Our dependence-upon God ought-to-be so entire and-absolute that-we should-never think-it-necessary, in-any-kind of-distress, to-have recourse to-human consolations. 11. He-who-would pass-the declining years of-his-life with peace and-comfort, should when young, consider-that-he-may-one-day become old, and-remember, when-he-is-old, that-he-has-once-been young. 12. I-would seek unto-God, and-unto-God commit my-cause. 13. The-integrity of-men is-to-be-measured by-their conduct, not-by-their profession. 14. He-who-has lost confidence can lose nothing-more. 15. Confidence in-conversation has-a greater share than wit. 16. The-conscience is more wise than science. 17. Man's conscience is-the oracle of-God. 18. He-is richest who-is content with-the least, for content is-the wealth of nature. 19. Reasonable men are-the-best dictionaries of-conversation. 20. Silence is one-great art of-conversation. 21. Fear God and-keep his commandments, for-this-is-the whole duty of man. 22. Gain may-be temporary and-uncertain; but ever while-you-live, expense is constant and-certain; and-it-is easier to build two chimneys than-to-keep one-in fuel. 23. If-a-good face is-a-letter of-recommendation, a-good heart is-a-letter of-credit. 24. The-worth of-a state, in-the-long run, is-the-worth of-the individuals composing it. 25. Liberality consists less in-giving much than-in-giving with-discretion. 26. The-human-race is-in-the-best condition, when-it-has-the-greatest degree of-liberty. 27. While-we-are reasoning concerning life, life is gone. 28. Love is incompatible with-fear. 29. Prudence and-love are inconsistent; in proportion as-the-last increases, the-other decreases. 30. The-most manifest sign-of wisdom is continued cheerfulness. (5 m 30 s).

371. He-is-happy whose circumstances suit his temper; but-he-is more-excellent who-can suit his temper to any-circumstances. (5 times in 1 m).

372.   TRANSLATE.

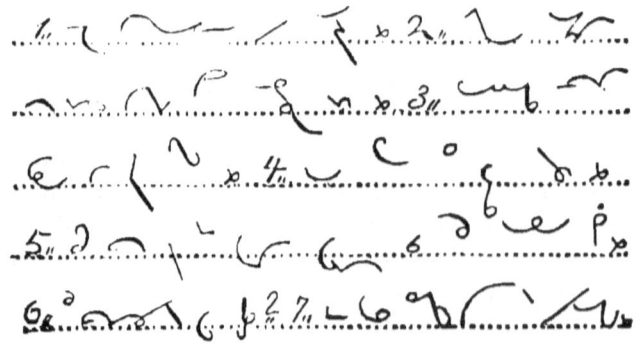

LESSON XXXII.

AFFIXES.

873.

Preserving castings himself lordship friendship courtship township admissable disgraceful	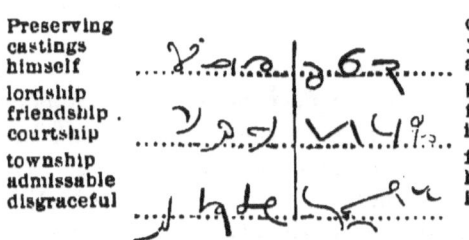	ourselves yourselves accountable barbarity fidelity instrumentality formality hospitality individuality.

874. The dot and tick are used to denote *ing* and *ings* respectively, in cases where the letter ⌒ ing cannot conveniently be joined, as in *preserving*, or *castings*.

875. The s and sez circles denote *self*, and *selves*, as in *himself*, and *ourselves*.

876. *Ship* is expressed by ish or shay, as in *friendship*. But in order to avoid unsuitable outlines, ish is sometimes disjoined, as in *courtship*, or *lordship*.

877. The endings *ility*, *ality*, and *arity*, are expressed by the detachment of any letter from the preceding part of the word, as in *barbarity*, *fidelity*, *instrumentality*.

878. The terminations *ble* and *ful* are often indicated by *be* and *ef* simply, as in *admissable*, and *disgraceful*.

879. In the list here given, the syllables printed in italics are represented by the signs just explained.

De*bility*, legi*bility*, fi*delity*, cre*dulity*, bar*barity*, for*mality*, vi*tality*, sta*bility*, instru*mentality*, famili*arity*, cas*ting*, obser*ving*, hus*tings*, disgrace*ful*, sensi*ble*, advisa*ble*, your*self*, it*self*, citizen*ship*; 1 pos. my*self*, thy*self*, divisi*ble*; 3 pos. our*self*, our*selves*, admissi*ble*, town*ship*. (Halving), hospi*tality*, individu*ality*, hard*ship*, lord*ship*, court*ship*, partner*ship*, accounta*ble*, ostensi*ble*.

380. EXERCISE 32.

1. The-more-a-man denies himself, the-more he-shall obtain

from-God. 2. He-that-has-never-known adversity is but half acquainted with others or-with himself. 3. No-sensible-person ever-made-an apology. 4. To-love-one-that-is great is-almost to-be-great one's-self. 5. Beauty, like truth-and-justice, lives within-us; like-virtue, and-like moral law, it-is-a companion of-the soul. 6. Man believes himself always greater-than he-is, and-is esteemed less-than he-is-worth. 7. Without content, we-shall-find it almost as difficult to-please others as ourselves. 8. No-man was-ever so-much deceived by-another as by-himself. 9. Dignity consists not-in-possessing honors but in-deserving them. 10. Economy is-of-itself a-great-revenue. 11. The-best and-highest part of-a-man's education is-that-which he-gives-himself. 12. The-more-you speak of-yourself, the-more-you-are likely to lie. 13. Do-you-wish men to-speak well of-you? Then-never-speak well of-yourself. 14. When-men are-friends there-is-no-need of-justice; but-when-men are-just, they still need friendship. 15. All-men would-be-master of-others, and-no-man is lord of-himself. 16. No-man is happy who-does-not-think himself so. 17. Self-trust is-the essence of heroism. 18. Think wrongly, if-you-please, but in-all-cases think for-yourself. 19. Do-not speak of-your happiness to-a-man less fortunate than yourself. (3 m 45 s).

381. Every-person has-two educations, one-of-which he-receives from-others, and-one-more-important, which he-gives-himself. (5 times in 1 m)

382. TRANSLATE.

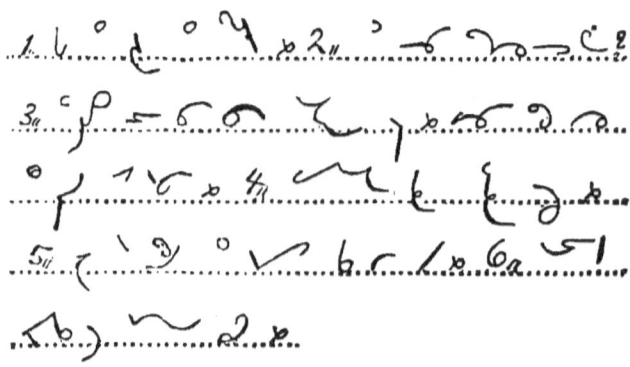

LESSON XXXIII.

EXPEDIENTS AND PUNCTUATION.

383.

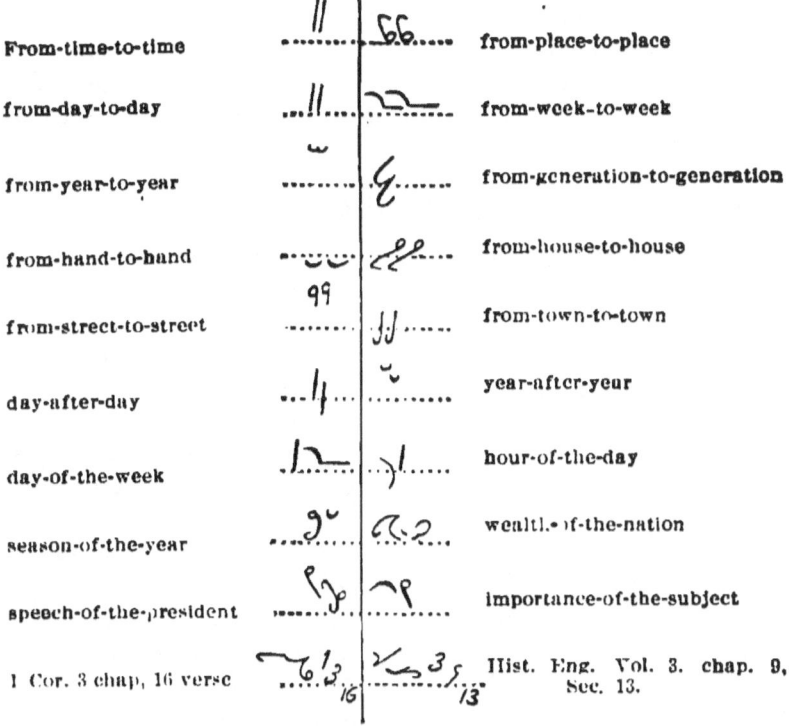

From-time-to-time	from-place-to-place
from-day-to-day	from-week-to-week
from-year-to-year	from-generation-to-generation
from-hand-to-hand	from-house-to-house
from-street-to-street	from-town-to-town
day-after-day	year-after-year
day-of-the-week	hour-of-the-day
season-of-the-year	wealth-of-the-nation
speech-of-the-president	importance-of-the-subject
1 Cor. 3 chap, 16 verse	Hist. Eng. Vol. 3. chap. 9, Sec. 13.

384. Only very common phrases, such as these, should be expressed by the expedients here made use of. In *some-of the-paper*, for instance, *of-the* should not be indicated by the nearness of *some* and *paper*.

385.   PUNCTUATION.

Parenthesis ... brackets

dash ... period

hyphen ... underscore.

386. Other punctuation marks are the same as in long-hand, but are rarely made use of except in correspondence. In reporting, a semicolon is indicated by a space of an inch or more. Little opportunity, however, is given for punctuating short-hand notes, the only practical method being to leave spaces to correspond with the speaker's pauses, and insert the proper marks afterwards when transcribing.

387.   EXERCISE 33.

1. It-has-been well observed that few are better qualified to-give-others advice than those-who-have-taken the-least of-it themselves. 2. Advice is seldom welcome. 3 Our happiness in-this-world depends-upon the-affections we-are-able-to inspire. 4. He-who-purposes to-be-an author, should-first-be-a student. 5. Books, like our-friends, should-be few, and-well chosen. 6. Every great-book is-an action, and-every great action is-a-book. 7. No-man-can-be brave who considers pain to-be the-great evil of-life; nor temperate, who-considers pleasure to-be-the highest good. 8. Judges and-senates have-been bought for-gold. 9. A-man's character is-the reality of himself; his reputation the-opinion others have-formed about-him; character resides in him, reputation in-other-people; that-is-the substance, this the-shadow. 10. The-scenes of-childhood are-the memories of future years. 11. Heaven lies about us in-our infancy. 12. It-is-better to-have-a lion at-the-head of-an-army of sheep, than-a sheep at-the-head of-an-army of-lions. 13. Conscience warns us as-a-friend before it punishes us as-a-judge. 14. Christ saw-much in-the-world to weep over, and-much to-pray over; but he-saw nothing in-it to-look on with contempt. 15. Knowledge of-our duties is-the-most

useful part of philosophy. 16. The-best education in-the-world is-that got by struggling to-get a-living. 17. Did-a-person but know the-value of-an enemy, he-would purchase him with-pure gold. 18. The-first and-last thing which-is required of genius is-the love of-truth. 19. Genius is-the gold in-the mine; talent is-the miner who-works and-brings it out. 20. Genius finds its-own road and-carries its-own lamp. 21. Hope is like a-bad clock, forever striking the-hour of happiness, whether it-has-come or-not. 22. The-setting of-a-great hope is like the-setting of-the sun. (4 m).

388. Phrase and punctuate: There are two ways of being happy we may either diminish our wants or augment our means either will do the result is the same and it is for each man to decide for himself and do that which happens to be the easiest if you are idle or sick or poor however hard to diminish your wants it will be harder to augment your means if you are active and prosperous or young or in good health it may be easier for you to augment your means than to diminish your wants but if you are wise you will do both at the same time young or old rich or poor sick or well and if you are very wise you will do both in such a way as to augment the general happiness of society.

389. TRANSLATE.

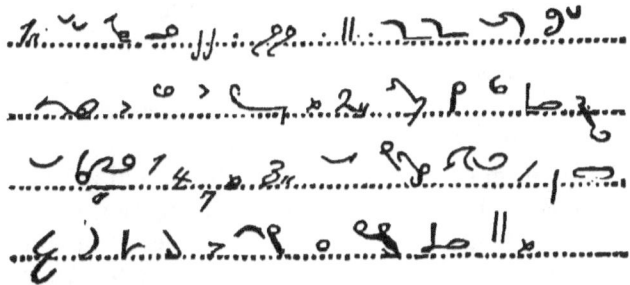

NOTE.—"Half the work of learning Short-hand consists in acquiring the ability to read without hesitation what has been written. Until one has acquired this ability, which long-continued practice alone can give, it will make no difference how plainly he may write, his notes will not be legible to him."

122   REPORTING STYLE OF SHORT-HAND.

LESSON XXXIV.

890.   **GENERAL PRINCIPLES.**

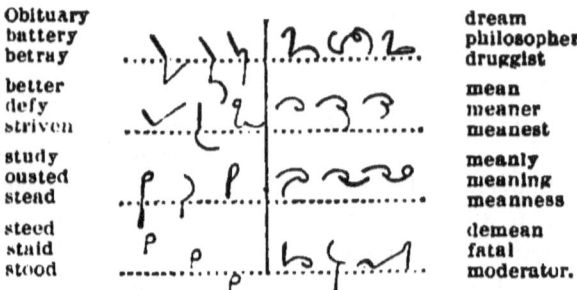

Obituary	dream
battery	philosopher
betray	druggist
better	mean
defy	meaner
striven	meanest
study	meanly
ousted	meaning
stend	meanness
steed	demean
staid	fatal
stood	moderator.

391. Since the consonant signs may be combined in numerous different ways, there arises an important question of choice concerning the various outlines which it is possible to construct for a given word, especially when unusual or technical terms and proper names are to be written. In *better*, for example, the consonant delineation, *b-t-r*, may be expressed by four different outlines, be-te-ray, be-te-ar, be-ter, and bet-ray. Which of these four best expresses the word? It will be observed that *b-t-r* is also the delineation for *betray*, which should, if convenient, be written differently from better. The first two are unnecessarily long; of the remaining two, the first properly expresses *betray*, and the last *better*, and for these reasons: In *betray*, be should not be halved to express te, since the rule is not to shorten any letter to express a te or de which belongs to a subsequent syllable. And, in this word, it is necessary also that the double consonant ter be used, since t and r coalesce, there being no intervening vowel. In better, expressed by the last outline, be is properly halved to denote the following te. The first two outlines read respectively, *battery* and *obituary*, and neither will admit of contraction, owing to the number of vowels to be supplied. In all cases the number and location of the vowels determine the precise outline to be selected, the rule

being that *every outline should be contracted as much as practicable but not be made so brief as to prevent vocalization.* This principle is further illustrated by the outlines chosen to represent words whose consonant delineation is s-t-d, *study, ousted, stead, steed, staid, stood.*

392. Each syllable of a word contains one vowel, and in order that this may be written, it is necessary that some of the preceding or following consonants be expressed with a long, or alphabetical sign. For example, in *de-fy* the alphabetic, rather than the adjunctive, or hook ef, must be written, in order that the vowel *i* may be inserted if necessary. This is important whether the vowel is actually written or not, since the use of the alphabetic, instead of the adjunctive sign, indicates that a vowel is to be supplied. In *striv-en*, for example, there are two vowels; hence there should be two long strokes, and no more. Of the first syllable consonants, te is the one properly chosen to be written long, in order that all the remaining consonant sounds, s, r, and v, may be expressed adjunctively. Hence is deducted the general principle, that *for each syllable of a word there must be either a full or half length alphabetic letter.* This, with the adjunctive signs that may be attached, is written with one stroke of the pen. There are, of course, many exceptions to this rule, as in case of words which have fewer consonants than syllables, as *o-bit-u-a-ry;* and others whose outlines will not admit of sufficient contraction, as *dream,* which contains but one syllable, but requires two strokes of the pen. But care should be taken as far as possible to so group together all the consonants in any one syllable, that they may be written at a single stroke, as in *phi-los-o-pher.*

393. Derivative words are commonly written by adding the necessary consonant signs to their primitives; e. g. the outlines for *meaner, meanest, meanly, meaning, meanness,* and *demean,* are formed by joining ar, est, el, ing, ens, and de, to the primitive mean. It is true that the most facile outlines are not always secured by conforming with this rule, as meanest, for example, could be more quickly written, em-nest. Nevertheless, this rule should be followed as long as angular outlines are the result, since by means of it, legibility is greatly increased, and the labor of acquiring the art considerably diminished. There are many exceptions to this, how-

ever, as when its observance produces unsuitable outlines, as in *druggist*, where to secure angularity, the st-loop instead of est, is joined to the primitive drug; also, where the syllabification is changed by means of the added consonants, as in *fa-tal*, (written ef-tel, not eft-lay), and *mod-e-ra-tor* (med-ray-ter, not med-ret-ar).

EXERCISE 34.

394. Words containing the same consonants, but requiring different outlines:

Spirit, separate, support; states, estates, status; stop, steepy, estop; caust, keenest, Kensett; trained, turned, tornado; browned, burned, brandy; spade, speedy, espied; skate, socket, asked; billed, blood, bloody; freed, afraid, forehead; deigned, dandy, denied; rend, around, ruined; older, ladder, Eldora; signed, assigned, synod; Elsie, Lucy, less; bayonet, bent, Bennett; married, humored, moored; scorn, screen, scrawny; estray, star, estuary.

TRANSLATE.

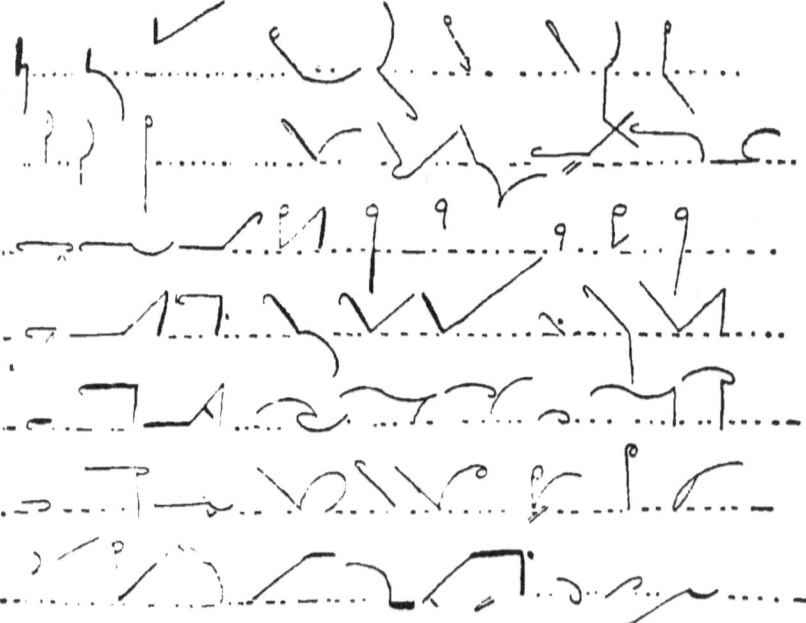

LESSON XXXV.

PROPER NAMES.

895.

A B C	P Q R
D E F	S T U
G H I	V W X
J K L	Y Z Washington
M N O	Carlyle Sherman Chambers
Porter Francis Montgomery Cumberland Morgan Ladd	Nelson Napoleon Foster Spencer Des Moines Iowa City

396. When practical, it is best to write proper names in both long and short-hand, particularly where the spelling is not indicated by the pronunciation. If in Court, for instance, Miss should be called as a witness, and her name written in short-hand only, the proper spelling, *Coralie Roth*, would not be known when the notes came to be transcribed. The stenographic character does not indicate the spelling of a name, but what is equally important, it gives the pronunciation, which the spelling of it does not do. Once writing in long-hand is sufficient for a name that occurs a number of times in a single report. If the spelling cannot be had, the name should be carefully vocalized the first time written. Names are so numerous that a vocabulary of them could not well be memorized; and this would be unnecessary, since the practical writer can readily invent sufficiently intelligible outlines for the most difficult of them. The halving principle should be made use of sparingly. Any outline which may stand for more than one name, as kay-per for both Cowper and Cooper, requires that one or more of the principal vowels be inserted. A name thus vocalized need not be underscored.

EXERCISE 35.

397.   FACULTY OF IOWA STATE UNIVERSITY.

J. L. Pickard, President, Nathan R. Leonard, Gustavus Hinrichs, Charles A. Eggert, Amos F. Currier, Stephen N. Fellows, W. F. Peck, P. J. Farnsworth, W. S. Robertson, W. D. Middleton, John C. Shrader, Leonard F. Parker, Elmer F. Clapp, P. H. Philbrick, Samuel Calvin, James M. Love, A. C. Cowperthwaite, W. H. Dickinson, George A. Thurston, Lewis W. Ross, Susan F. Smith, Emlin McClain, Austin Adams, John F. Duncombe, John N. Rogers, C. M. Hobby, I. P. Wilson, James H. Rothrock, W. D. Stillman, William C. Preston, Thomas H. McBride, Phebe Scofield, Will E. Crane, O. T. Gillett, T. G. Roberts, Chas. W. Eaton.

398. Cowper, Channing, Byron, Drummond, Harrington, Hudson, Beecher, Dickens, Evans, Harrison, Lambert, Blackstone, Clay, Douglass, Cobden, Everett, Hale, Herbert, Andrews, Brewster, Bacon, Brown, Butler, Chapman, Clinton, Franklin, Hamilton, Hedge, Lincoln, Luther, Macaulay, Mitchell, Osborn, Pascal, Potter, Rochester, Rogers, Ruskin, Spurgeon, Strickland, Taylor, Tennyson, Thompson, Wesley, Irving, Johnson, Littleton, Liverpool, Madison, Monroe, Buchanan, Logan, Newton, Nellie V. Hutchinson, Lillian Cooley, Bessie Gardner, Wm. A Shepfer, Chas. R. Brown, A. A. Ladd, Will H. Miller, H. W. Seaman, H. C. Truesdale, Jas. B. French, Clara Gruber, Emil L. Boerner, Fred. A. Remley, W. H. Martin, Frank Olds, Myron E. Wheeler, Lyman Banks, Emma Searles, Ada Gaston, Marion Grayson, Jenny Griffiths, Lide Cameron, London, Edinburgh, Paris, Berlin, Philadelphia, Boston, Denver, Lexington, St. Paul, Omaha, Lancaster.

SPECIAL RULES AND PRACTICAL SUGGESTIONS. 127

399. TRANSLATE.

LESSON XXXVI.

SPECIAL RULES AND PRACTICAL SUGGESTIONS.

400. Exceptions must sometimes be made to the rules given for the proper curving and slanting of letters to prevent certain outlines from expressing too much; e. g. *assail* and *jail* are written in the manner shown by the first and third outlines, not by the second and fourth.

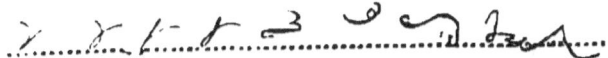

Assail   jail   gravest nicest Northampton Trans-Continental Ry. Co

401. Est may sometimes be struck upward, as in *gravest*, and *nicest*.

402. Reporters often contract the outlines for such lengthy words and phrases as *Northampton*, or *Trans-Continental Railway Company*, especially if these are repeated several times in one report.

403. The liquids *r* and *l* are commonly expressed by ray and lay, ar and el being employed only when their use secures more angular or facile outlines. Final *l* when preceded by ⌒, ⌒, ⌒, or ⌒, should be expressed by the downward stroke. When this letter follows an initial vowel, el should be used, as in alike (el-kay);

but exceptions are made when necessary to secure angular outlines, as in *alight*, written lay-te, instead of el-te. Shay is employed only when ish cannot be, which is rare, as in shell, written shay-lay, not ish-lay, or ish-el. Shay and el are never used standing alone.

404. The professional reporter is allowed certain licenses, which should not, however, be taken by the student. In rapid writing, he may give the letters less than the required amount of slant or curvature, omit shading to a certain extent, and even in some cases write first and third position words on the line. Every writer in time becomes familiar with those inaccuracies which are peculiar to himself; but it should be his constant aim to keep as near the standard as possible, in order that the legibility of difficult passages may not be endangered, and, also, that others may be able to read his notes.

405. Limit of inaccuracy. In no case, however, should a word be written so far wrong as to appear to be an entirely different word.

406. The greatest speed will be gained ultimately, only by writing the characters quite near each other, and cultivating as small and neat a hand as possible.

407. No stenographer can afford to disregard certain general directions which relate to the mechanical part of his profession. He should use paper distinctly ruled, and of the best quality only. A good fine pointed, short-nibbed gold pen of medium size should be employed. This should be more or less elastic, dependent on the writer's lightness of touch. Arnold's writing fluid is most suitable.

408. If a pencil is used, it should be of medium hardness only, kept sharp, and used with soft or uncalendered paper. It is well to employ this only in exceptional cases, since the transcribing of pencil notes is injurious to the eyes. For various other reasons, also, the pen is much superior to the pencil for short-hand work.

409. Professional stenographers commonly use note-books manufactured expressly for this purpose. Not only are these the most suitable for such work, but greater ease of writing is secured by the habitual use of books which are uniform as to size of page, width of ruling, and quality of paper.

410. All stenographic notes, no matter for what purpose taken, should be filed, indexed, and carefully preserved for several years.

The contingencies are many which may render a transcript of some portion of these very valuable.

EXERCISE 36.

411. THE BOLTER SCHOOL BILL.

Extract from a speech delivered before the Iowa Legislature by Hon. R. L. Bolter, Feb. 26, 1884. Reported by F. A. Remley.

1. Mr. Speaker:—The-important-changes proposed are in-the 1st, 5th, and 157th Sections of-this-bill. 2. It-will-be readily seen on-a careful examination, that-in-these three Sections will-be-found all-the real changes. 3. What-are-these-changes? 4. Simply, sir, that-each civil township is made-a corporate body for school-purposes, having-the-right to sue and-be sued, and-do-other corporate acts. 5. Now, I-am-aware, sir, that-this fact alone, in-my-judgment, will elicit about-the-only discussion that-will be called out by-the-bill. 6. Each civil township is-the smallest-governmental division of-our State and-National system, and-has-been in-existence since colonial times. 7. Every school boy of-twelve understands their boundaries. 8. If-I were asked to-explain the-present school-system, and-our abominable system of-school-districts, I-would-be unable to-do-so. 9. I-think-it-is-not-too-much to say that-not-one-of-my-friends will-be-able-to-explain to-this House the-system for-which he-will contend. (2 m).

NOTE.—"In taking down rapidly the words of another, no time is allowed for giving any attention to the principles of Grammar, Punctuation and Capitalization. Knowledge of these, however, is absolutely necessary in making an acceptable transcript. It will not do to write out a speech or a letter as though it were one long, loose sentence, without a pause or a capital in it. Inability to readily capitalize, punctuate and re-arrange poorly constructed sentences will and should debar one from the profession. To give satisfaction the young reporter must be able carefully to correct all obvious grammatical errors made by the speaker, insert the proper marks of punctuation, capitalize the right words, and to divide the whole into appropriate paragraphs."

LESSON XXXVII.

AMANUENSIS REPORTING.

412. As a prerequisite to success in this field, a thorough education is demanded in the common English branches, as arithmetic, orthography, grammar, and business forms. Good penmanship, and a knowledge of type-writing, book-keeping, and in rare cases telegraphy and some of the modern languages, are also valuable.

413. Various degrees of speed, ranging from 90 to 150 words per minute, are required. As such secretary, it becomes one's duty to write letters, telegrams, contracts, agreements, newspaper articles, briefs, editorials, etc., at the dictation of his employer, or whoever has the business management, and afterwards transcribe and deliver the same. A better understanding of the secretary's duties may be gained from a consideration of the relations existing between him and his employer. It is much more severe mental work to rapidly indite important business letters, than to slowly write them out. Dictating is in fact as much an accomplishment as reporting. Perfect quiet, and security from all disturbance, are essential in the work of dictating letters and papers of this kind. Hence the stenographer to the fullest extent possible, should refrain from everything that may perplex or disconcert the reflections of his superior. He should not only maintain quiet, but be prepared the moment called upon to read what he has written, and remain in constant readiness to record every word spoken. He should also abstain from all show of nervousness during the occasional intervals in the dictation.

414. When the matter in hand is entirely finished, he may ask for the spelling of proper names, insert words which he failed to hear or record, and make the necessary corrections. Apparent grammatical and verbal errors need not be called up, but should be corrected by himself when the transcript is made.

EXERCISE 37.

415. 1. The-best time to-frame an-answer to-the-letter of-a-friend is-the-moment you-receive-it. 2. Then-the-warmth of-friendship, and-the intelligence received, most forcibly co-operate. 3. Letters which-are warmly sealed are-often but coldly opened. 4. Let-your-letter be-written as accurately as-you-are-able,—I-mean with-regard-to language, grammar, and stops; for-as-to-the matter of-it, the-less trouble you-give-yourself the-better it-will-be. 5. Letters should-be easy and-natural, and-convey to-those-to-whom we-send-them just what we would-say if-we-were-with-them. 6. To-write a-good love-letter, you ought-to begin without-knowing what-you-mean-to say, and-to-finish without-knowing what-you-have written. (1 m 30 s).

---

416. OMAHA, NEB., DEC. 3, 1883.
William Tackaberry & Son,
    Sioux-City, Iowa.

GENTLEMEN:—We-understand the-impression has-been-formed by-you that E. C. Palmer & Co. have-been given the-agency in-your-city for-our crackers.

We-beg to advise you that-such-is-not-the-case. We-do-not purpose to-give the-agency for-our crackers to any-one-house, thereby depriving ourselves of-a vast amount-of business we would otherwise get. We-have-been offered the-exclusive trade of-other wholesale-houses in-your-city for-that privilege, but have-always declined and-in future will pursue the-same policy.

We-beg-to advise you further that the-advertisement given us by Messrs. Palmer & Co. in-their journal, is-entirely gratuitous. They-are-not recompensed either directly or indirectly for-the-same by-this-house.

We assure-you your business is thoroughly appreciated by-us, and-will-always meet with as-much favor at-our hands as any-house trading with us, either in Sioux-City or-elsewhere.

        Yours respectfully,
            JOS. GARNEAU CRACKER CO.
Dictated to Miss Ada Gaston. (2 m. 30 s.)

417. St. Paul, Minn., Nov. 8, 1883.

Messrs. A. Ruiz & Sons,
   Malaga, Spain.

Gentlemen:—Referring-to-your esteemed favor of-the 21st ult., we-wish-to say, that-when-you-are ready to quote prices on-your brands of layer raisins, we would-be-pleased to-receive quotations, with-the view of-placing our fall-and-winter order with-you. We would also kindly request you to inform us whether-you-have any arrangements with-any line of steamers running from-your port to New-York or Baltimore, and-what rates of freights you-can quote us; also, what-the insurance and-other expenses connected with-a shipment of say 5,000 or 10,000 boxes would-be. Any-other information that-you-can-give-us, that-you-think would-be valuable for-us, will-be appreciated. Awaiting your reply, we-are
   Very-truly-yours,
      Glidden, Griggs & Co.

Dictated to W. A. Shepfer.   (1 m 45 s).

---

418.   Nebraska Hospital for the Insane,
         Lincoln, Neb., Nov. 20, 1883.

J. W. Trisler,
   St. Louis.

Dear-Sir:—Mr. Trisler was brought to-the Asylum a-few months ago from Wyoming Ter. He-is-insane, but quiet, and-in-general good-health. My-impressions are-that-he-will-not recover his mental health soon, probably never. He-is comfortable, and-seems-to-be contented. At any-time, if-you-would-like to-hear from-him, just drop me a-postal-card, anything to-remind me, and-I-will take-pleasure in writing-you.
         Respectfully,
            H. P. Mathewson, Supt.

Dictated to Miss B. Archibald.   (1 m).

419. ST. PAUL, MINN,, Feb. 29, 1884.
D. Getty & Co.,
    White Bear, Minn.

GENTLEMEN:—Enclosed I hand-you statement of-your account to Jan'y 1st. You-know we-do-not-often say-anything to-you about-money, but just-now we-are-having heavy demands upon-us, and-collections are rather slow, so-that we are compelled to ask-you to-do all-that-you possibly can for-us. We-shall greatly appreciate anything you-can-do.

                                   ALLEN, MOON & CO.
Dictated to Will E. Miller.   (1 m).

---

420.   TRANSLATE.

FARR & Co., Collection, Real Estate and Insurance Agents.
                                CEDAR RAPIDS, IA., Dec. 12, 1883.

Mr. Doolittle,
    Marshalltown, Io.

421. NEBRASKA HOSPITAL FOR THE INSANE,
LINCOLN, NEB., NOV. 20, 1883.

Mr. F. J. Dowd,
Hastings, Neb.

LESSON XXXVIII.

AMANUENSIS REPORTING, (Continued).

422. The thoughtful student need not be told that, since all the plans and secrets of his employer's business must be made known to the correspondence clerk, the most implicit confidence is reposed in him, and loyalty, integrity, and devotion to business are presumed by the relationship established. He should not only be so discreet as not to divulge office secrets, or betray implied confidence, but he should show plainly by his conduct that he is **faithful** to his employers, and interested in their behalf.

423. No matter how accomplished a private secretary may be, his services will not be sought, if he has not cultivated **habits of** prudence, and shown himself to be safe and **trustworthy**.

424. In taking difficult matter at dictation, in which corrections and interlineations are afterwards to be made, it is well to leave the alternate lines blank for this purpose. Letter books should be paged, and every letter indexed in a separate book in such a manner that it can be quickly referred to afterwards.

EXERCISE 38.

425. Nebraska Hospital for the Insane,
Lincoln, Neb., Nov. 20, 1883.
Hon. E. J. Hainey,
Aurora, Neb.

Dear-Sir:—Mrs. Crarger is very insane, and-is-inclined to-be violent and-troublesome. I-think her-friends would-find her very-difficult to-manage. Doubtless it-would-be desirable to-the County, and-it-certainly would-be to us, to-have her off our hands; yet-it-is-my-opinion that-it-would be-a-very unjust proceeding, both to Mrs. Crarger and-her-friends, to-place her in-a private family. We get-along with-her very-well, and-with-very-little trouble, but I-feel-certain that-if she were with-persons not accustomed to-manage the-insane, they would-find it-impossible to-get-along with her. However, if-the Commissioners of Insanity think-best to-try-the experiment, certainly there-could-be-no-objection on our-part; yet I wouldn't advise it.

Respectfully,
H. P. Mathewson, Supt.
Dictated to Miss B. Archibald. (1 m 45 s).

426. Farr & Co., Collection, Real Estate and Ins. Agents,
Cedar Rapids, Iowa, Dec. 4, 1883.
Mr. M. Traver,
Le-Grange, Ill.

Dear-Sir:—Yours of Nov. 30th received. You ask if-I-have-a lot of-good-farms for exchange? I-have-not at-the-present-time a-large list for exchange, but-some for-sale. I-might possibly get-you an-exchange on-farm or good town property in Cedar Rapids,

or in-North-Western Iowa. Will write-you-again soon–and tell-you-what-I-have. Yours-truly,
MARK C. FARR.
Dictated to Anna Goodell. (1 m).

---

427. ST. PAUL FIRE AND MARINE INS. CO,
ST. PAUL, Jan. 4, 1884.
Albo De Bernales, Esq.,
New York.

DEAR-SIR:—Replying to-your favor of-the 19th inst. we herewith enclose statement showing amount of-the grain premiums, as-they-have-been reported to-you under-our grain series. The-amounts reported in-October and-November grain account have-been paid to-you, and-the-balance will-be included in-Dec. account. If-you-cannot find reports for these by examining your files, we-will send-you duplicates. We-are-quite certain that-we-have-sent-you reports for-all of-these risks as-soon-as received by us. Yours-truly,
Stenographic Letter. C. B. GILBERT, SEC'Y.
Dictated to Bessie Gardner. (1 m 20 s).

---

428. GEO. W. CRANE & CO.,
Blank-Book Manufacturers, Printers and-Binders,
Mr. A. B., TOPEKA, KAN., March 20, 1884.
Los Angeles, Cal.

DEAR-SIR:—The-Dockets sent-you are-the-kind which-are in-general use in-this-city. The-full printed form made it-necessary in-a-great-many-cases to transfer the-record to-the-back of-the-book. This-is obviated in-the-form which we-send-you, and-also in-the Justice's Guide which we enclose, and-which will give-the Justice the-form of entry of any case that-may-come before-him. We-will exchange the-Docket if-you-wish, but think-your Justice will-find the-form sent the-more convenient.
Yours very-truly,
CRANE & CO.
Dictated to Lide Cameron. (1 m 30 s)

429. OUR HOME ON-THE HILLSIDE,
DANSVILLE, LIVINGSTON CO., NEW-YORK, March 1, 1884.

Isaac Bennett, Esq.,
   Carrollton, Ill.

MY-DEAR-SIR:—Our mutual-friend, Mr.-Peters, who-is-at-present in-the-employ of-Our Home on-the Hillside, as-one-of-its reporting-secretaries, has handed me your-letter of Feb. 20, wherein you express a-desire to-have-my testimony in-respect-to stenographic-writing. It gives-me great-pleasure to say-to-you, that-for twenty-six years I-have-had young-men-and-women in-my-employment as stenographers. Such-is-my estimate of-the-value of-the-art of-short-hand, that-I-would-have-it taught in-all-our graded-schools and-academies throughout the-land to young-men-and-women. Taking all-our institutions into account, and-the wide range of-occupations in-which-our young-men have-to engage, and-which-are opening to-our young-women, I-would-rather have given proficiency in stenography as-a-part of-a young-man's or-a young-woman's education, than-the-best average Collegiate accomplishment which any-of-our Colleges or-Universities furnish in-the Latin and-Greek languages. It-is-not simply as scribes for-others that-this-art is-of-value; for-it-is of-quite as-much service to-those-who attain it in-their-own private affairs. What-an-excellent opportunity it furnishes to-one who-has-it at-hand to-make memoranda of things seen and-heard, and-thus furnishing him with-the-means of-fastening in-his mind, and-having at-his service, most useful information! I-have-had on-an average for twenty-five years, not-less-than three short-hand-writers in constant use; and-I-do-not-know of any who after my training have-not secured good-positions, and-kept them, and-obtained entirely satisfactory compensation. Assuring you that-I-am in-the fullest sense a-believer in-the-worth of-the-art as-a-means of added usefulness in-whatever profession or-calling any-person may-be engaged, and-wishing you all-success in-your pursuit of-it, I-remain,   Yours faithfully,
                    JAMES C. JACKSON.
                         (5 m).

430. TRANSLATE.

GLIDDEN, GRIGGS & Co., Importers & Wholesale Grocers,
ST. PAUL, MINN., Nov. 9, 1883.

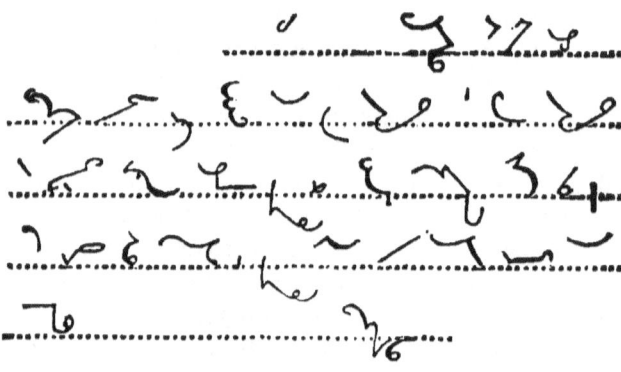

---

431. JOS. GARNEAU CRACKER CO.,
OMAHA, NEB., Dec. 3, 1883.

432. ST. PAUL FIRE AND MARINE INS. CO.,
ST. PAUL, Jan. 15, 1884.

Mr. G. E. Schwindt,
Kimball, D. T.

LESSON XXXIX.

SPEECH REPORTING.

433. A verbatim report of a rapid public speaker is the greatest achievement of the stenographic art. There are, however, but comparatively few speeches of which reports are wanted; and it is a fortunate fact that the best orators, whose speeches are the most frequently published, are the easiest, also, to report. But it is very rare that a speech appears well in print, in the precise language in which it was delivered. A certain amount of tautology and repetition add to the force of a spoken address, which in a printed report must be discarded. Many allusions, and even whole sentences, may oftentimes be profitably omitted; and the rhetoric of an extemporaneous speech can generally be improved. These matters lie clearly within the scope of the stenographer's duty; but the best plan is always, when possible, to submit to the speaker himself an exact copy, written on paper with a broad margin, in order that he may amend and remodel as he sees fit.

434. The student will find the following suggestions of value, whether he intends making a business of this branch of reporting or not.

Fully prepare yourself before the speech begins. Obtain a seat, one at a desk if possible, within easy hearing of the speaker. Have yourself amply provided with writing material. Use a pen, if you are accustomed to one; otherwise, have a number of sharpened pencils at hand.

435. No matter what the purpose of your report may be, make it a point, far as you are able, to take every word that is uttered. If the entire speech is not wanted, you can prepare an intelligent synopsis from your full short-hand notes; but an abridgement made in short-hand while the speech is being delivered, is by no means satisfactory.

436. Beginners are sometimes obliged, however, before they can follow a rapid speaker, to make as full a synopsis as they are able, recording the substance only of what is said. And it is commonly the case, indeed, that only partial reports of very rapid speakers are wanted.

437. A complete report of a speech requires that many things be inserted, which, verbally, are not a part of the address itself, things acted rather than said. The manner and appearance of the speaker should be described; also, the character of the audience, and the demonstrations of approval, or otherwise, with which the speaker's utterances are received.

EXERCISE 39.

438. 1. As-it-is-the-characteristic of-great wits to say-much in-few words, so-it-is of-small wits to-talk much and-say-nothing. 2. It-is-when you-come close-to-a-man in-conversation that-you discover what-his real abilities are. 3. Speech-making is-a knack. 4. Men are-born with-two eyes, but-with-one tongue, in-order-that-they should see twice as-much-as they-say. (1 m).

489. THE-PRESENT-AGE.—CHANNING.

1. The-remarks now-made on literature might-be extended to-the fine-arts. 2. In-these we see, too, the-tendency to-universality. It-is-said, that-the-spirit of-the great artists has died out; but-the taste for-their works is spreading. 3. By-the improvements of engraving, and-the invention of casts, the-genius of-the great-masters is going abroad. 4. Their conceptions are no-longer pent up in galleries open-to but few, but meet us in-our homes, and-are-the household pleasures of millions. 5. Works designed for-the halls and-eyes of emperors, popes, and-nobles, find their-way, in no poor representations, in humble dwellings, and-sometimes give-a consciousness of-kindred powers to-the child of poverty. 6. The-art of drawing, which lies at-the-foundation of-most of-the fine-arts, and-is-the-best education of-the eye for-nature, is-becoming-a branch of-common education, and-in some countries is taught in-schools to-which all-classes are admitted. 7. I-am reminded by-this remark of-the-most striking feature of-our times, as showing its tendency to-universality, and-that-is-the unparalleled and-constantly accelerated diffusion of-education. This greatest of-arts, as-yet little understood, is making sure progress, because-its principles are-more-and-more sought in-the-common nature of man; and-the great-truth is spreading, that-every-man has-a-right to-its aid. 8. Accordingly education is-becoming-the-work of nations. 9. Even in-the despotic governments of Europe schools are open for-every child without-distinction; and-not-only-the elements of-reading and-writing, but-music and-drawing are taught, and-a foundation is laid for future progress in history, geography, and-physical science. 10. The-greatest minds are at-work on-popular education. 11. The-revenues of states are applied most liberally, not-to-the universities for-the few, but to-the common-schools. 12. Undoubtedly much remains-to-be-done; especially a-new rank in-society is-to-be given to-the teacher; but even in-this-respect a-revolution has commenced, and-we-are beginning to-look on-the guides of-the young as-the chief benefactors of-mankind. (4 m).

440. TRANSLATE.

Spiritual Freedom—

LESSON XL.

CONVENTION REPORTING.

441. Stenographers are employed to report the proceedings of various deliberative assemblies, as legislatures, constitutional, and the more important political conventions, and professional and trades-men's associations. These reports are commonly furnished to newspapers, and also frequently published in book form. The purposes for which they are made, and the degrees of fullness required are so various, that no comprehensive rules can be laid down sufficient to govern the reporter in every case. The following suggestions, however, will be found of value.

442. The stenographer should if possible be seated near, or at the same table with the official secretary, in order that, as the business progresses, he may learn the names of speakers, and those taking part in the discussions.

443. It is the best plan always to take as full notes as possible although an abridged report only may be wanted, since the work of condensing can better be performed when the transcribing is being done, than when the proceedings are in course.

444. It is commonly the reporter's duty to take down all motions and resolutions, except those in writing; also, amendments thereto, and remarks and decisions thereupon.

445. Essays, and other papers which are read to the association, are filed with the secretary, and need not be taken down in short-hand; but the discussion of any question to which these may give rise, should be noted by the reporter.

446. The speaker's name, when announced by the chairman, should be written in long-hand at the left margin of the paper, and his remarks recorded just below.

447. The official stenographer of the convention should make a record of everything that transpires. Much revision, and the judgment of an editor, are needed in preparing such verbatim reports for publication. This is usually done by the secretary, or a special committee. Short-hand writers experienced in this

branch of the profession, are often employed both to make and revise, or edit, such reports.

EXERCISE 40.

448. PROCEEDINGS

OF THE

THIRD ANNUAL MEETING OF THE IOWA STATE PHARMACEUTICAL ASSOCIATION,

HELD IN DES MOINES, FEBRUARY 14-15, 1882.

OFFICIALLY REPORTED BY ELDON MORAN.

FIRST DAY.—WEDNESDAY AFTERNOON SESSION.

The-meeting was called-to-order at 10 o'clock. President Hogin in-the chair.

The-minutes of-the last session were read, corrected, and-approved.

The-President: I-will-now call-for-the-report of-the Committee on Legislation.

The-report was read by-the Chairman, Mr. Bush, and-the paper passed to-the Secretary.

On motion of Mr. Wallace, the-report of-the Committee on Legislation was adopted.

The-President: Dr. Treat, have-you any-thing-further to-report on Pharmacy and Queries?

Dr. Treat: Yes-sir: a-paper by Mr. W. H. Hardy, of-Clinton.

The-Secretary: Mr. Chairman, I-would-like-to-say first, that our Treasurer has-a-letter from Mr. Hardy, expressing regrets for-his inability to-be at-the meeting.

The-President: We-will-now listen to-the reading of-the paper by Mr. W. H. Hardy, of Clinton.

The-paper is read to-the Association by Dr. Treat.

The-President: Now-you-have heard-the reading of-the-paper by Mr. Hardy, of-Clinton. What-is-the-pleasure of-the house as-to-the disposal of-it?

Dr. Treat: I move you Mr. Chairman, that the communication be received.

The President: You mean by that, that it shall be printed in the proceedings?

Dr. Treat: Yes sir.

The motion was carried and the thanks of the Association tendered the writer.

Mr. Schafer: I will now present the report of the committee appointed to consider the Presidents address.

Vice-President Townsend assumes the chair.

The committee referred to report as follows: "To the President and members of the Iowa State Pharmaceutical Association: Your committee appointed to consider the address of our retiring President, ask to present the following report:

We do most heartily concur in the leading suggestions. We would, however, call your special attention to the following recommendations:

1. That every registered Pharmacist look well to all impositions from unprincipled persons, in obtaining liquors for improper use under all manner of representations.

2. That we heartily endorse the aiding and sustaining the Commissioners of Pharmacy in their duties to the full extent of the law.

3. The subject of revising the By-Laws had our attention, but owing to the necessities of the case, amendments have already been adopted, which fully cover this point.

4. We most heartily and cheerfully endorse the suggestion, that the Association become incorporated under the laws of the State. A motion to adopt the report of the committee prevailed.

Mr. Crawford: Mr. Chairman; I move you that the Committee on Legislation, as expressing the sense of this Association, be instructed to procure an amendment to the present law, making it a penalty not exceeding $200.00 for a person conducting a pharmacy without registration, by having that matter so that it will properly come before the Grand Jury, and that the Court may act at discretion, and make a fine not exceeding this amount. There are communities where the prohibitory liquor law of Iowa is practically a-dead-letter. No Grand-Jury can-be impaneled to-take proper cognizance of-the law.

The-law-maker makes-the law, not-only to-rule subjects, but-also to-rule the-law-makers. Now I-think-that, in-this-matter, we-stand between-the law-maker and-the law-breaker. In-this-respect we-are handling, unfortunately, patent medicines, one-of-the giant evils of-the day. That-there-is-a-demand for-them, no-one questions. This-demand comes as-well from-the law-maker as-it does from-the law-breaker. While-one-man claims to-call-for-it within-the limits of-the law, there-is-a-question at-last about-what there-is-a-call-for. Now-then, we-are-not only standing between law-makers and law-breakers, but-we-stand between-the patent medicine man and-the consumer, between-the physician and-the patient. It-seems-to-me our-position is-a-very peculiar one. For-instance, some nostrum is placed upon-the market and-it-is so advertised that-there-is-a-demand-for-it, and-we, as retail-dealers, purchase some and-sell it to-our-customers who-demand-it. It-is-a spurious article. Who-gets-the blame? I-think-those-who-are doing-business on-honest principles and-living up to-the law, will go forward and-raise the-standard so-high that-every-one will-be ashamed to engage in-that-business.

The-President: The-motion now is-that-the Committee on Legislation procure a-pharmacy law making-the violator liable to-a penalty not-exceeding $200.00.

Mr. Parish: Did-you-say-that-it-should-be indictable?

Mr. Crawford: Yes-sir. I-said-that-it-should-be-a **misde-meanor**, and-that-the penalty should-be-that-amount.

A-Member: I-think-there ought-to-be-a way of-getting out-of it without-making it a-Grand-Jury affair. I-think-it-is-an **offense** that ought-to-be punishable before-a-justice-of-the-peace.

Mr. Parish: I-don't-think, Mr. Chairman, that-you-can-find-a town in Iowa, where-there-is-a druggist, but-who-has-a delicacy about filing-a complaint against-a competitor. But if-you-make-it a-Grand-Jury offense, they-will-be obliged to-take action in-these-matters. You-may take-it in-any town. There-is one in-our town who-is-not-a pharmacist, not eligible by-reason-of age, and-he-is violating the-law, and-there ought-to-be **somebody** whose duty it-was to-take action in-these-matters.

CONVENTION REPORTING. 147

Mr. Ellis: Let-us-take-a view of-our position as druggists, the-position in-which we-are held up before-the-public, so-far-as we-are individually concerned. It-ought-to-be our object personally to abide by-the-laws, whatever these laws may-be. (11 m).

449. TRANSLATE.

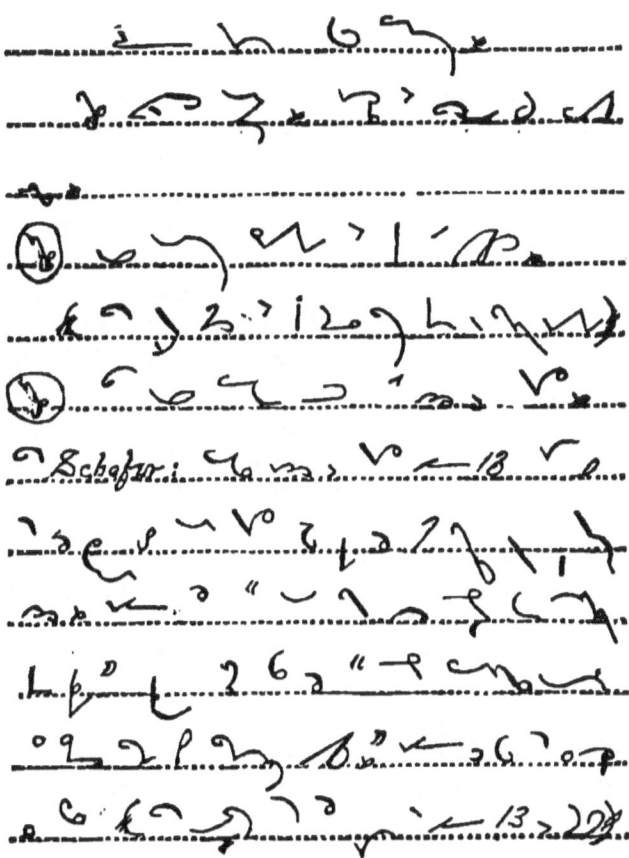

NOTE.—The successful reporter of public meetings is wide-awake and observing; on the alert constantly not only to hear what is said, but to know what is meant by the speaker. The Stenographer who does not know the meaning of what he writes cannot be relied upon to make a correct transcript.

LESSON XLI.

LAW REPORTING.

450. Law Reporting, or the business of recording the proceedings had on the trial of causes, is one of the most important branches of the stenographic profession. In this day, all the more important cases are reported in short-hand, and, indeed, of so great advantage is this art found to be in the administration of justice, that in many states the appointment of skilled stenographers is authorized by law. In the most perfect methods of administering justice that have been devised, it has been required that some kind of record of the evidence be preserved, and the fuller this is the better.

451. Stenography has revolutionized the methods of proceeding in the Courts; for by its *speed* much time is saved, and delays, which, during a trial, are prejudicial to justice, are more easily prevented, and the occasion for expensive re-trials oftentimes precluded. In no business or profession is stenography more welcome than in law, where so much depends on a record being kept of the precise words made use of.

452. The Law Reporter must possess various qualifications in order to a competent discharge of the duties of his calling. He should be able to write at least one hundred and seventy-five words a minute, and read his notes fluently. In addition, also, to a thorough English education, good memory, and quickness of perception, he should have a familiar acquaintance with the various forms and methods of proceeding in Courts. The greater his knowledge of law, especially that of evidence, the better. No student should neglect the main features of this branch of the profession. Especially the forms of such reports should be learned, since amanuenses, and all short-hand writers in fact, are frequently desired to make reports of depositions, referred cases, and the testimony received at preliminary hearings.

453. The *Caption* of a law-stenographer's report should show the title, number, and nature of the cause, the Court where pending, the name of the judge, referee, commissioner, or other tribunal by whom the same is heard; the term of court, building, town, county, and state where the trial is had; the name of counsel appearing on either side; the name and address of the stenographer employed. This should occupy the first page and be drawn up in the following manner:

454. CAPTION.

JAMES MORGAN, et al.
vs.
OSCAR A. SIMONS
and
JOHN H. BASS.

No. 789.

APPEARANCES:
NINDE & ELLISON,
Attorneys for Plaintiffs.
R. S. TAYLOR and
COOMBS, MORRIS & BELL,
Attorneys for Defendants.

EJECTMENT.

Pending in the U. S. Circuit Court for the Northern District of Indiana, June Term, A. D. 1881. At the Federal Court room, Fort Wayne, before his Honor Judge Walter Q. Gresham, and a jury.

ELDON MORAN, Official Stenographer,
Indianapolis, Ind.

455. The report proper begins on the second page, the heading of which should show for what party litigant the testimony is taken, the hour, the day of the week and month, and the year, when the trial was begun. Names of witnesses should be written in longhand. The record should also show what attorney conducted the examination.

456. The main body of a law-report consists in the record of question and answer, or what is said by the lawyer in eliciting testimony, and by the witness in reply thereto. That which is spoken by the lawyer is for convenience denominated *question*, and the reply of the witness, *answer*, although the reverse is sometimes in fact true, as may be illustrated by the following colloquy between lawyer and witness-

Ques. (lawyer) Where were you living at the time?
Ans. (witness) When do you mean?
Ques. (lawyer) I mean at the time the accident happened.

457. Paper about five inches broad is the most convenient for law-reports. The question begins at the left margin and extends across the page. The answer should begin, and be entirely written, in such a manner as that no part of it shall be nearer than one and one-half inches of the left margin. Answers, when brief, may be written on the same line with the question, providing a space of at least one inch is allowed to intervene.

The proper heading, and disposition of question and answer, is illustrated by the exercise for translation at the close of the lesson.

EXERCISE 41.

458. TESTIMONY OF JACOB FRY,—*Continued.*

Q. You-may state-what-was the-condition of-the bank at-the-time Robinson built the-dock if-you-recollect. First state as-to-the surface of-the ground.

A. It-was like all-other canal-banks. A-sluice ran through there—was banked up-and stopped up with logs, for-the culvert to-go-through.

Q. Where-the Robinson-House now-stands, what-was-the natural lay of-the ground?

A. Well up in-some-places; but all-the-waste water ran in next the-canal there, and-the creek ran-down there-also.

Q. Where-the Robinson-House now-stands, you-say-the-ground was up? What-do-you-mean, that-there-was-a knoll, or hill?

A. Yes-sir, a-knoll used-to-be-there.

LAW REPORTING.

Q. How-is-the low place now, as compared with-its-condition then?
A. There-is-a sort of hole or pond.
Q. Where-was-the pond?
A. Where-it-is-now, before-the-dock went-in.
Q. How-far south of-where-the dock now-is, did-the basin then-come—what-they call-the-basin?
A. About-as-far-as it-is-now.
Q. What-business did Robinson carry on-there?
A. He owned-a shoe-shop, and-afterwards started a-tan-yard.
Q. Where-were-the vats?
A. All-along under-his whole building.
Q. Where-was-the north-end of-the-building?
A. Where-it-now-stands, after-he-had-it all-built up; he-had tan-vats clear up to-the-canal.
Q. Do-you-recollect any-building being west of-the Robinson-House—any-other-business there?
A. A-saleratus factory.
Q. Who-was-that owned by?
A. By Tyler.
Q. Do-you-remember the-year in-which Mr. Robinson built-the docking?
A. No-sir. (3 m).

ALWAYS BE ON TIME.—"There is no other one thing that will do more towards commending a person to the favor of people in general than promptness in attending to his duties. This is the case in every kind of business, but it is especially true of the reporter. In most occupations in which a person is doing business for himself he may frequently neglect it by tardiness and no one be the loser but himself. With the Stenographer, however, there is more of other people's interest dependent upon him than in almost any other position filled by subordinates. If he is employed in the courts, or is to make a report of some speech or convention, he may, by not being on time, cause these to be adjourned for the day, involving the loss, it may be, of hundreds of dollars worth of time and, what is far worse, lose his reputation as a prompt and reliable reporter, which, when once lost, will be hard to win back again."

459. TRANSLATE.

EVIDENCE ON PART OF PLAINTIFF.

TUESDAY, JUNE 15, 2 P. M.

Jacob Fry,—sworn. Examined by Mr. Ellison.

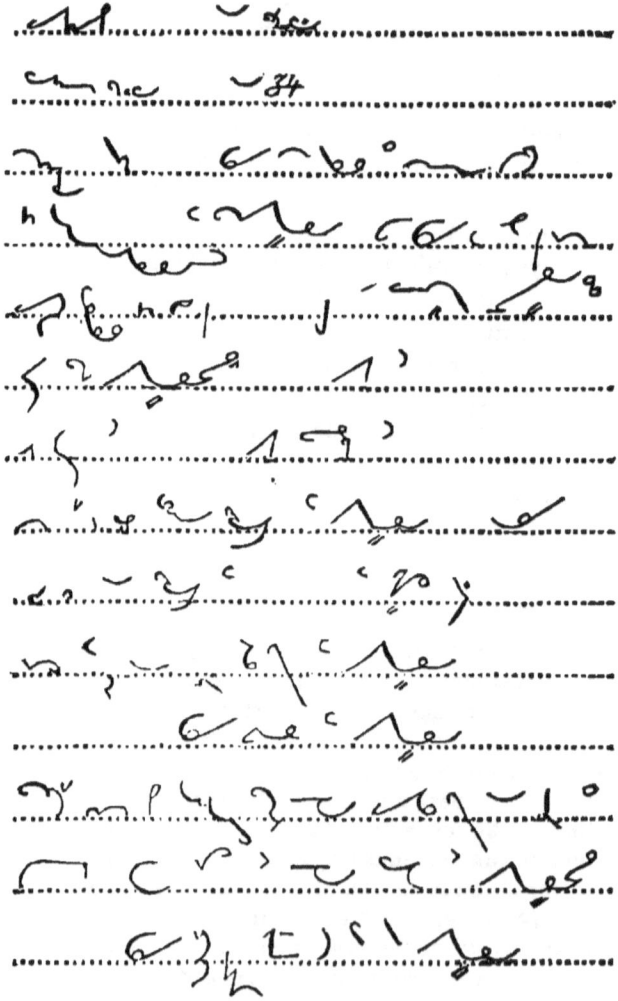

LESSON XLII.

OBJECTIONS, RULINGS, AND EXCEPTIONS.

460. The main purpose in reporting a law-suit, is that the party aggrieved may be secured in his right of appeal to a higher Court. There are many other uses, however, which these records are made to serve. A verbatim report is useful in various ways on re-trials, as, for instance, when impeachments are sought; also, to refresh the memory of counsel and witnesses, and settle disputes in regard to the testimony formerly elicited.

461. For the same reasons they are often serviceable in collateral proceedings; also, to perpetuate the testimony of witnesses who subsequently decease or become insane. Even during the trial, the presence of "Mr. Reporter" has grown indispensable, as shown by the fact that his notes are hourly referred to.

462. The stenographer's notes are presumed to be correct, and cannot be changed or modified except with the consent of the judge, and agreement of interested parties. The record should contain, not only everything that is said pertaining to the trial, but by whom it is spoken. When questions are asked, or remarks made, by the Court, jurors, or attorneys not conducting the examination, or by the parties themselves, the name of the speaker should appear, parenthetically, in the margin.

463. Next in importance to the evidence itself is the recording of objections, which are made from time to time to the introduction of the same, or to any proceeding which either party may regard as illegal. The grounds upon which such objections are based should be noted by the reporter; and should they not be stated specifically, the counsel's argument in presenting the matter to the Court should be taken down. When an objection is decided, the exception, if any, taken by the party overruled, should also be recorded. Exceptions are also taken to the decisions of the Court in sustaining or overruling various motions submitted in the course of the trial.

464. In reporting depositions, objections are recorded, and testimony taken subject thereto, no rulings being made, or exceptions taken, at the time. A law-report should be as nearly as possible a *photograph* of all the proceedings had. Hence, it becomes the reporter's duty to make a minute of every transaction which has a bearing on the case. Examples of such notes which are inserted parenthetically are, "Witness refuses to answer the question," "12 o'clock M. Court adjourns," "The railing referred to by the witness is about twenty feet distant," "Gentleman referred to by witness is Mr. Jones, attorney."

465. In some civil and most criminal cases, a report is made of the impaneling of the jury. This should embrace the examination of each juror as to his qualification to act, challenges peremptory and for cause, by both prosecution and defense, rulings of the Court, and exceptions of counsel.

466. The reporter is at liberty at all times to check witnesses who speak too rapidly or indistinctly, or while the question is being put, or objection made.

EXERCISE 42.

467.

WILSON H. SWALES, Guardian, *vs.* THE WHITE-WATER RAILROAD COMPANY.	No. 1460.	APPEARANCES: HOLMAN & McMULLEN, *Atty's for Plff* BELL & BAINBRIDGE, *Atty's for Deft.*

DAMAGES.

Tried at Lawrenceburg, Indiana, at the May Term A. D. 1881 of the Dearborn County Circuit Court, before his Honor Judge Hayes, and a jury.

ELDON MORAN, Official Stenographer, Indianapolis, Ind.

Charles Ashby,—sworn on the part of Plaintiff.
Examined by Mr. McMullen.
Q. Where-do-you-reside?

A. In Harrison Township, Dearborn Co., Ind.
Q. Do-you-know where Longnecker station is?
A. Yes-sir.
Q. Tell-the-Jury where-you-live in-reference-to-the station.
A. I-live on-the pike about-one-quarter of-a-mile from-the-station. Right about here, (referring-to-the map, exhibit "B").
Q. How-far is-it from-where-you-live straight across to-the railroad?
A. About forty rods.
Q. Do-you-remember when-this accident happened?
A. I-believe it-was-the 9th of December, 1879, between five and six o'clock, to-the-best of-my-knowledge.
Q. You-may state-whether it-was light or-dark.
A. It-was on-the darkish order. It-was-a sort of cloudy evening.
Q. How-far is-that from-where-the railroad crosses into Franklin County?
A. About two-miles.
Q. Where-were-you on-the evening that-this-accident happened?
A. At my house, standing out on-the porch.
Q. What-did-you first hear,—not what-was-said to-you—; first state-whether-or-not you-heard any collision or noise?
A. I-heard-the collision, that-is what drew my-attention.
Q. State to-the Jury whether-or-not at-this-time you saw-the passenger-train.
A. I-did.
Q. Where-was-the passenger-train when-you saw-it?
A. It-was coming along-down here by-the dam.
Q. Where-did-the work or wild train whistle if-at-all?
A. Right-here at-the graveyard—just-gave one blast.
Q. You-may state-whether-that work-train gave-another signal from-that-time till-you-heard the-collision down by-the crossing.
A. Yes-sir, that-is-all I-heard till-the-collision.
Q. Now how near was-this train to-the passenger-train when-the-passenger moved away-from the-station?
A. Well, I-cannot answer that because-I-cannot see-the station from-my house.

Q. Was-there any-time when-you-could see both trains at-once?

A. Yes-sir, when-the-passenger-train was here in front of-the graveyard, (referring-to-the map), the-wild train was coming around-the dam.

Q. Tell-the-Jury about-how-far apart these trains were at-that-time.

A. Considerably over-a-mile.

Q. That-is, when-the-passenger-train was-at-the graveyard?

A. Yes-sir.

Q. How-far down toward-the-station could-you see-the passenger-train from-your-house?

A. To-right above-the target at-the upper end of-the switch.

Q. How-far above-the-railroad is-this ground where-your-house is located?

A. Forty-five feet I should-judge.

Q. How-long-was-it from-the-time-you-heard-the whistle till-you-heard-the-collision?

A. I-didn't pay any-attention, but it-was-a-very-short-time.

Q. Have-you any-thing by-which-you-can measure the-time?

A. No-sir, I-didn't pay-much attention at-that-time. It-was so short-a-time that-I-made remarks to-my wife—

Q. If-you-have-any-thing by-which-you-can fix it in-your-mind without telling what-was-said-and-done, you-may-give us your-best knowledge of-it.

A. It-was-a-minute or somewheres about-there; perhaps it-might-have-been that-long or-longer to-the-best of-my-knowledge.

Q. Did-you-go down to-the station after-that?

A. Yes-sir, they came after me just-a-few-minutes after-it happened, a-very-short-time.

Q. You went-down then?

A. Yes-sir.

Q. Who-went-with-you, if-anybody?

A. Nobody went with-me, only-the-gentleman who-came for-me.

Q. Were-you there when-the-train backed up again?

A. No-sir.

Q. Had-it gone on when-you arrived?

A. It-was just-going when-I-got-there.

Q. Where-was Miss Hurley?
A. Right at-the end of-the crib.
Q. What-was done with-her?
A. She-was picked up and-carried to-my-house.
Q. How-long did she remain at-your-house?
A. I-think two-or-three days.
Q. Did-you ever measure the-distance between-that crib and-the railroad?
A. I-measured between-the end of-the shingle-pile and-the rails; I-think the-distance was-about one-hundred feet.
Q. You did-not measure the-crib by-itself?
A. No-sir, but I should-judge the-crib to-be about sixty feet long.
Q. It-is simply a-pile of shingles with-a shed over it?
A. Yes-sir, that-is-it.
Q. Can-you see-the crossing from-your-house?
A. No-sir, I-cannot.
Q. Now-suppose a-party is seated in-a two horse spring-wagon, the hind wheels being-past this-end of-the shingle-shed, how-far above-the crossing can-the-railroad target be-seen?
Mr. Bell objects-to-the-question, as calling for-a-conclusion of-the witness rather-than for-the facts. Question withdrawn.
Q. I-wish-you-would state just the-condition of-the lady, when-you saw her there at-the-time-when she-was-taken-up to-your-house.
A. She-was perfectly unconscious, did-not-know-anything-for-a couple of-days.
Q. What bruises, if-any, did-you see upon her?
A. She-had-a wound on her arm, but I-do-not-remember now which-one; she-had also-been struck on-the head.
Q. Where-was-the wound dressed? A. At-my-house.
Q. Who-was-the physician? A. Dr. West, of Harrison.
Q. Was she-taken-away from-your-house before she again-became conscious?
Mr. Bell, on-part of-defendant, objects-to-the-question on-the-ground that-it-is leading. Objection sustained. Plaintiff-excepts.
Q. Did she go away from-your-house, before or-after-she-became conscious?

158   REPORTING STYLE OF SHORT-HAND.

Mr. Bell on-part of-defendant objects-to-the-question on-the-ground that-it-is leading, incompetent, and-immaterial. **Question withdrawn.**

Q. Did-you ever work on-a railroad? A. No-sir.
Q. Have-you any-judgment as-to-the speed of-trains? A. No-sir.
Q. You-may state in-your-judgment, whether-the wild-train was-running faster or slower than-the passenger-train.

Mr. Bell objects-to-the-question on-the-ground that-it-is-incompetent. Objection sustained. Plaintiff-excepts. (11 m).

468.

CROSS EXAMINATION OF CHAS. ASHBY.—BY MR. BELL.

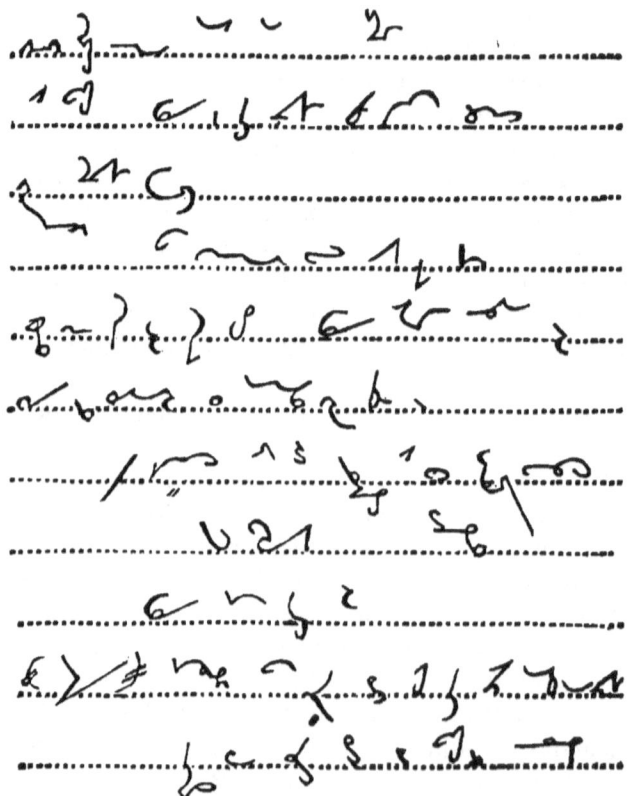

LESSON XLIII.

EXHIBITS AND INDICES.

469. Written documents, as deeds, notes, contracts, mortgages, letters, depositions, etc., are frequently produced in Court, and made a part of the evidence; and for the purpose of identification, and convenience in making references, the same are at the time marked by the reporter as exhibit "A", "B" etc., according to the order in which they are introduced. After the alphabet has been exhausted, the double letters "AA", "BB" etc., may be employed. The paper, besides the letter "A", should be marked with the initials of the parties to the suit; thus, for example, in the case of Frederick vs. Wilson, the certificate of a County Auditor is offered in evidence, and marked by the reporter Exhibit "A", F. vs. W. This prevents ambiguity in cases where the same document has already been marked with a different letter, as an exhibit in another case.

470. As part of the evidence, also, knives, rings, keys, photographs, or any article whatever which it may be important for the Court and Jury to examine, are from time to time introduced. These may be marked by attaching a written card firmly to them. The reporter should be careful to identify as an exhibit, every article or document *offered* by either party, whether or not the same is actually *admitted* in evidence by the Court, since rejected exhibits are necessary to complete the appellant's bill of exceptions.

471. Half the value of a law report is lost by not having it properly indexed. In the first place, the paper used should be accurately paged, and each separate book or manuscript numbered in the order used. Trials vary in length from an hour to several months. Reference is frequently made, and the reporter ordered to read sections of testimony taken days and even weeks previous. This can be done only by means of a *running index*, which is kept making from hour to hour, just as the proceedings take place. This should give the *day* and *date* of each session of Court, the *name* of each *witness*, and the *page* where his testimony and cross-examination begins.

472. Agreements, admissions, stipulations, and the introduction of exhibits, should also be indexed. Long-hand transcripts are paged and indexed in a similar manner.

INDEX.

473. SWALES
 vs.
THE WHITE-WATER RAILROAD. } EVIDENCE ON PART OF PLFF.

FIRST DAY, MAY 19, 1881.

THURSDAY FORENOON SESSION.

Impaneling of the Jury, Vol. 1, Page 1.
M. B. Fox, ... " 1, " 5.

AFTERNOON SESSION.

Fox, continued,	. .	1–11	Chas. Ashby, ...	1–37
Cross-examination,	. .	1–13	Cross-ex., ...	1–42
Re-direct examination,		1–20	C. Ashby, recalled, . .	1–48
Frank Jackman, . . .		1–22	Benj. Holden, ...	1–48
Cross-ex., ...		1–28		

SECOND DAY, MAY 20.

FRIDAY FORENOON SESSION.

B. F. Hurley, ...	1–59	Guardianship, admitted	2–3
Cross-ex., ...	1–63	Exhibit "B", Map of Long-	
W. H. Swales, . . Vol.	2–3	necker, admitted . .	2–4
Exhibit "A", Letters of			

FRIDAY AFTERNOON SESSION.

Cross-ex., ...	2–4	Dr. L. J. Collins, . . .	2–28
Carrie Hurley, ...	2–15	Dr. J. P. Green, . . .	2–44
Cross-ex., ...	2–21	Dr. J. D. Gatch, . . .	2–47

THIRD DAY, MAY 21.

SATURDAY FORENOON SESSION.

EVIDENCE ON PART OF DEFENDANT.

Mrs. M. Jackman, . . 2-52 E. F. Lamon, . . . 2-54

SATURDAY AFTERNOON SESSION.

H. Barneclo, ... 3-15 E. H. Bowlby, . . . 3-26

FOURTH DAY, MAY 23.

MONDAY AFTERNOON SESSION.

Dr. W. H. Myers, . . 4-52 Ashby, admitted . . 4-74
W. W. Worthington, . 4-68 Exhibit "D", Statement of
Exhibit "C", Statement of Jackman, admitted . 4-74

REBUTTING EVIDENCE ON PART OF PLAINTIFF.

Mrs. Jackman, recalled, 4-75.

EXERCISE 43.

474. SWALES
           vs.   } IMPANELING OF-THE JURY.
THE WHITE-WATER R. R. CO.

Mr. McMullen, on-part of-Plaintiff:

GENTLEMEN - OF - THE - JURY : — This-is-a-case in-which Dr. Swales, who-is-the guardian of Miss Hurley, is-the-plaintiff, and-the White-Water R. R. Co. is-the defendant, being-a-suit brought for-damages, and-for-an alleged injury sustained by Miss Hurley, the-plaintiff's ward. Have-you, Gentlemen-of-the-Jury, heard anything of-this-case? If-any-of-you have heard anything-about-it, please-make-the fact known.

(Jury make-no response).

Q. Did anybody with-whom-you-have talked pretend to-give-you the-facts?

(Juror) Well I-heard this-about-it—

Q. Did-the-person with–whom-you talked say-that-he-was telling you the-facts in-the-case?

A. No-sir, I-think-not.

Q. Then-have-you formed or-expressed any-opinion as-to-whether the-plaintiff should recover in-this-case?

A. To-the-best of-my-knowledge I-don't believe I-have. I-was going-to say-that I-had-not-heard of-the suit until I-came to-the city. To-the-best of-my-recollection I-have-not expressed any-opinion.

Q. Mr. Keed, have-you-heard of-the-case before?

A. Yes-sir, often.

Q. Heard of-the facts?

A. Yes-sir, and-expressed my-opinion of-the-case when-it occurred; I-live close there and-know-all about-it.

Q. And-you-have-formed and-expressed an-opinion about-it?

A. Yes-sir.

Q. Do-you-think your-opinion would-have-any influence upon-you in-making-up-your verdict?

A. Yes-sir, I-think-so.

Q. Do-you-think-you-could-render a-verdict in-this-matter upon sworn testimony of-witnesses here-upon trial independently of-your-own-opinion?

A. No-sir, I-think-not. I-have already expressed my-opinion.

Upon motion Mr. Keed is excused from-the-Jury by-the Court.

(Mr McMullen) Your-Honor, we-pass the-Jury.

Upon-the peremptory challenge of-the defendant, the Court excuses Mr. Stone from-the-Jury.

By Judge Bainbridge, on-part of-the Defendant:

Q. Mr. Hart, have-you-heard of-this-case?

A. Yes-sir.

Q. Heard what purported to-be-the-facts in-the-case?

A. Yes-sir, I-both heard and-read about-it at-the-time the accident happened.

Q. Have-you-formed any-opinion as-to-the merits of-the-case?

A. Yes-sir.

Q. Already have-your-mind made up?

A. Yes-sir, to-a-certain-extent.

Q. Is-your-opinion such-a-one as would readily give way to-sworn testimony?

A. Well I-think-it-would.

Q. Can-you-say positively that-the opinion that-you-have already formed would-not in-a-measure influence your final verdict?
A. I-don't-think-that-it-would.

Defendant's challenge of Mr. Hart for cause is over-ruled by-the Court, to-which ruling defendant-excepts.   (4 m).

475.   INSTRUCTIONS TO THE JURY.

John B——.
   vs.   } IN THE DISTRICT COURT, BUTLER CO., NEB.
Conrad M——.

Gentlemen-of-the-Jury: 1st. This-is-an-action brought by-the-plaintiff against the-defendant for-damages which-the-plaintiff alleges he-has sustained by-reason-of-the defendant having falsely and–maliciously (it-is-charged) in-the-presence and-hearing of divers good-people, who understood the-German-language, spoken and-published of-and concerning the-said-plaintiff certain words in-the-German-language, which-would in-the English-language mean, "He (meaning-the-plaintiff) stole my lath out-of-the chicken house." The-defendant denies he-spoke such-words of-and concerning plaintiff, but justifies the-speaking of-the-words, and-claims that-plaintiff did steal his lath, and-that plaintiff did-not sustain a-good-character among-his neighbors for-moral-worth, integrity, and-honesty. The-plaintiff denies in-his reply these new matters in-defendant's answer. 2nd. The-Court instructs the-Jury that slander is regarded in law a-malicious wrong and-injury, and-an-action for-it has-as legitimate a-standing in-a-Court as-any-other-action. 3rd. All-questions of-fact you-will-determine for-yourselves from-all-the evidence and-circumstances of-the-case. 4th. If-you-believe from-the-evidence that-the-defendant, in-speaking of-the-plaintiff, in-the-presence and-hearing of-others who understood the-German-language, used-the-words charged in-the petition in the German language, meaning-in-the English-language, "He (meaning-the-plaintiff) stole my lath out-of-the chicken house," then it-will-be-your duty to-find for-the, etc.

Given at David City, Neb., Dec. 4, 1883, by Judge Norval.
   Myron E. Wheeler, Official Stenographer.   (3 m).

476. SWALES
vs.
THE WHITE-WATER R. R. Co. } TESTIMONY ON PART OF PLFF.

Wilson H. Swales,—sworn.

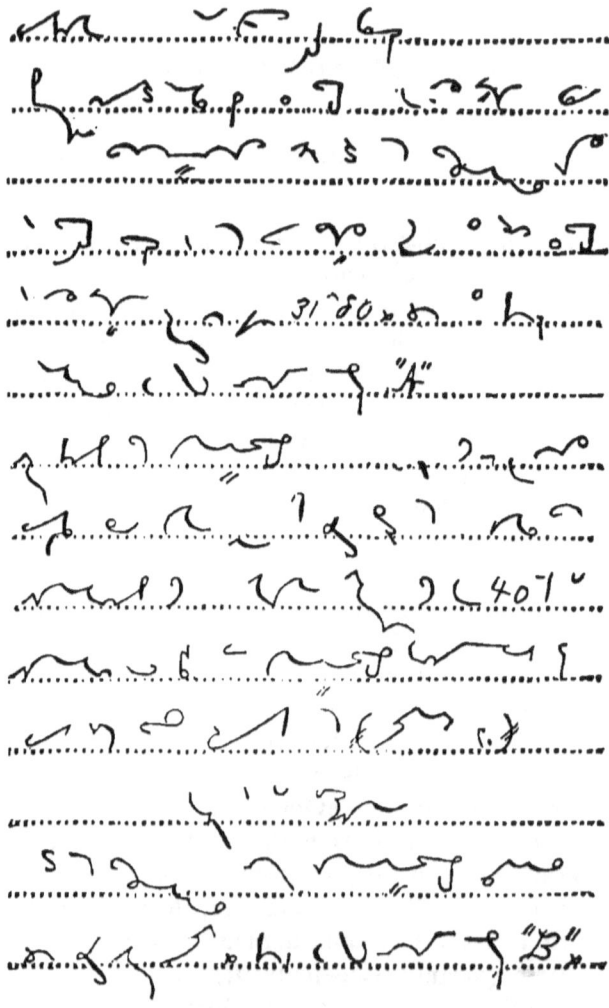

LESSON XLIV.

TRANSCRIPTS.

477. All short-hand reports should be securely filed away, either by the Clerk of the Court, or by the stenographer himself. A transcript in long-hand may be ordered at once, or not till after years; possibly never. Before making such transcript, the reporter would do well to ascertain whether more than one copy is wanted, since, should he make use of a type-writer, which is much the best plan, two or more copies can be made simultaneously. The testimony of certain witnesses only, or a brief of all the evidence in narrative form not containing objections, etc., is sometimes ordered; while again, only an abstract is wanted, giving the testimony to which objections were made, together with the rulings and exceptions. In addition to the usual fee allowed for making transcripts, the reporter receives extra compensation for the work of making such briefs and abstracts. In all cases, the stenographer has a right to hold the transcript until his fees are paid.

478. Original notes are always taken hurriedly, and need more or less revision and condensation when transcribed into long-hand. In this matter the reporter is allowed some discretion. Answers of witnesses with few exceptions should be written as spoken, but the language of interrogatories should be corrected if ungrammatical, and may be abbreviated often with advantage. Lawyers not uncommonly indulge in repetitions which have only the effect of lumbering the record, and should in many cases be entirely excluded from the transcript.

479. Notes should be transcribed in the order taken, and one side only of the paper be written upon. Ample margin for the notes of counsel should be allowed to remain at the left of each page; also at the top, so that the sheets may be bound together.

480. Every interrogatory should be numbered, beginning anew with the testimony of each witness. The transcript, when complete, is paged and indexed, and bound firmly into volumes of convenient size.

481.

STATE OF INDIANA } CROSS-EXAMINATION OF MRS. RACHEL STOWE,
vs.   *Continued.*
LYON.

482. TRANSCRIPT.

STATE OF INDIANA }   H. W. HARRINGTON,
                 }   on part   Prosecution.
     vs.   }   DANIEL W. VOORHES,
    LYON.   }   for *Defendant.*

CROSS-EXAMINATION OF MRS. RACHEL STOWE, *Continued.*

Ques. 31. How far were you standing from the corner tree when you heard the report of the pistol?

Ans. About as far from it as I am from the stove there (referring to the stove about sixteen feet distant).

Ques. 32. You say you heard two shots; now was it a long or short space of time that elapsed between them?

Ans. It seemed to me rather long.

Ques. 33. Well, how long?

Ans. Perhaps a minute.

Ques. 34. Are you certain as much as that?

Ans. Yes sir, that long anyway.

Ques. 35. Will you please indicate the time that elapsed as nearly as you can remember it, by tapping with my knife upon the desk?

(Mrs. Stowe taps twice; time, eighteen seconds, by the reporter's watch).

Ques. 36. How far was your boy standing from you at the time?

Ans. About as far away from me as that gentleman, (referring to Senator Voorhes).

Ques. 37. Were not remarks passed between you and the boy during the time between the shots?

Ans. Yes sir, my boy first said ———— Objection.

Ques. 38. Did not he know one of the men on horse-back, and did not he say "He has shot ————" ?

Mr. Griffith objects to the question on the ground that it is not proper cross-examination; also, that it misrepresents the witness.

Objection overruled. Defendant excepts.

EXERCISE 44.

483.

[Heading, Question and Answer, Objections, etc., to be arranged by the student in the proper manner].

Benj. T. Frederick vs. James Wilson. Appearances: Timothy Brown, Attorney for Contestant. J. H. Bradley, Attorney for Contestee. Contested Election. For the office of Representative in Congress for the Fifth District of Iowa. Cause pending in the House of Representatives of the United States of America. Testimony taken before Eldon Moran, Stenographer and Commissioner, during the months of February, March, April, and May, 1883. Evidence on part of Contestant. Session at Marshalltown, Iowa, March 5, 1883. A. N. French, sworn on-part of contestant. You-may-state if-you-are-the Auditor of Marshall-County, Iowa, and-have-now in-your possession the-poll-books which-were returned to-you from Washington Township? Yes-sir, I-am Auditor, and-have-them. Please-take-the poll-book, and-read so-that-the Commissioner can-take-it-down, giving the-number of-votes that-were cast in-that Township for-each-Candidate for-Congress at-the November-election 1882. I-understand you-want-the certificates just-as they-were returned? Yes-sir. For Representative-in-Congress there-were 110 votes cast, of-which James Wilson had 45; Benj. T. Frederick 52; and David Platner 13. Is-that-the-number of-votes for-each-Candidate returned in-the abstract made by-the County canvassers to-the Board of-State-canvassers? Yes-sir, the-same-number. Please-turn to-the poll-book of Marietta Township and-state how-many-votes were returned from-that township for-the office of-Representative-in-Congress by-the Trustees of-that township, as-shown by-the poll-books, and-read it off so-that-it-may-be taken-down by-the Commissioner. (Reading from poll-book.) For-Representative-in-Congress, Fifth District, there were 123 ballots, of-which James Wilson had 81; Benj. T. Frederick 37; and David Platner 5. Please-turn to-the poll-book of Le-Grande Township, and state how-many-votes were cast for-each Candidate at-the-last November-election, for-the office of-Representative-in-Congress, Fifth District. (Reading from poll-book.) For-the office of-Representative-in-Congress, Fifth District, there-were 263 ballots cast, of-which James Wilson had 180; Benj. T. Frederick 78; and-David Platner 5. Now state if-your returns made for Washington, Bangor, and-Marietta Townships, were-the-same as-shown by-the-poll-books. I-will-have-to-look and-see. First, I-will-ask-you, if-you-have-a copy of-the returns made by-the County canvasser to-the State-canvasser? Yes-sir, I-have. Now state as-to Washington Township, how-many-votes for-the office of-Representative-in-Congress were returned to-the State-canvassers for-this Township. For James Wilson 45; B. T. Frederick 52; David Platner 13. Now state with-reference-to Marietta Township. James Wilson 81; B. T. Frederick 37; David Platner 5. These numbers correspond with-the poll-book. State, also, with-reference-to Le-Grande Township. The schedule shows James Wilson received 180 votes; B. T. Frederick 78; and-David Platner 5. These numbers are-the-same as-those I-read from-the poll-book. Now state with-reference-to Bangor. For-the office of-Representative-in-Congress, there-were 85 ballots cast, of-which James Wilson had 75; B. T. Frederick 2; and-David Platner 12. The-abstract also shows Wilson to-have-received 75; Frederick 2; and-Platner 12. Excused. (5 m).

SUGGESTION.—"As soon as you are able to apply all the principles correctly, you can not do better than to make all your memoranda in short-hand. This will be of help to you in several ways. It will develop confidence in your work, a thing which most beginners are very apt to lack. By making note of items upon which something of importance depends, and trusting wholly to your notes for them, you will soon find yourself feeling just as certain of their meaning as you would were they written in long-hand, a feeling you must have if you would make a successful reporter. Another advantage to be derived from such a habit is the constant practice which it gives. The greatest advantage, however, of forming the habit of using short-hand in making memoranda is in the fact that, since it can be done so easily and rapidly, one is far more apt to note down many little things which, were it necessary to write them out in long-hand would be neglected altogether."

LESSON XLV.

PROFESSIONAL CONDUCT.

484. The reporter should be prompt in his attendance upon Court, and in the preparation of transcripts; diligent and accommodating as an officer.

485. It is not unusual for him to be made the confidant of the Judge, and for this reason he should exercise the greater caution, since he is the more subject to interested inquiry. He is expected to make a true and impartial record; and, to avoid all inference of prejudice, it is by far the best policy to say nothing whatever about the case during the trial. He should be trustworthy, and mix suavity with discretion.

486. In the heat of an exciting trial, when the feelings and apprehensions of adverse parties are most awakened, the slightest look, movement, or insinuation on the reporter's part, is liable to be construed into an indication of prejudice or partiality. The utmost care and circumspection are necessary to prevent such reflections, which are sometimes carried even to the extent of a question as to the integrity of the report.

EXERCISE 45.

487.

FREDERICK *vs.* WILSON

TIMOTHY BROWN,
  Atty. for Contestant.
J. H. BRADLEY,
  Atty. for Contestee.

EVIDENCE ON PART OF CONTESTEE.

Session at Marshalltown, Iowa, April 12, 1883.
James K. Johnson, sworn. Examined by Judge Bradley.
Q. What official-position if-any do-you hold?
A. I-am deputy-clerk.
Q. Have-you-examined-the naturalization records of-this-county?

A. Yes-sir, also all-the-records of naturalization that-have-been kept by-the Circuit and-District-Courts.

Q. Have-you-made-a-memorandum of-what these-records show concerning-the naturalization of-certain-persons?

A. I-have.

Mr.-Brown on-part of Contestant objects to-the testimony of-this-witness on-the-ground that-it-is incompetent and-immaterial, the-original record books only being admissible as-evidence.

Q. I-will-ask-your attention to-the declaratory statement made by James Dunn. State-whether-you ever examined the-record of-the naturalization of-such-a-person, and-if-so, when-did-you find that-it-was-made?

Mr.-Brown on-part of Contestant objects-to-the-question on-the-ground that-it-is incompetent and-immaterial. The-original books themselves are-the-best evidence, and-the witness should-not-be-allowed to-testify from any-document other-than these-books themselves.

A. I-have examined-the-records carefully, and-find that-there-are two James Dunns. One made-his declaratory statement on-the 28th of July, 1856; the-other made-his declaratory statement on-the 12th of-Dec., 1866. I-also found from-a careful examination of-the naturalization records of-the District and-Circuit-Court Journals from-the-beginning, that-is, from Journal A down to-the time-when-the naturalization records were begun, that-there-is-no record of James Dunn's having-been naturalized.

Mr.-Brown on-part of Contestant objects-to answer of-witness on-the-ground that-it-is incompetent and-immaterial, since-it purports to-be-a statement of-the official records, the-same not-being produced.

Q. Then we-understand you as testifying that-there-is-no record of any second-papers ever-having-been issued to any-such-person?

A. No-sir.

Q. To any James Dunn, or James Dunn, Jr.?

A. No-sir.

Q. What-do-the records show with-reference-to Patrick Dunn?

A. On-the 27th of-August, 1866, Patrick Dunn made-his declaratory statement, but-there-is-no record of-his ever-having-been naturalized.

Mr.-Brown on-part of Contestant moves that-the-answer be-stricken out as incompetent and immaterial, being-the statement of-what-the-records contain, without-the-same being produced.

Q. No-evidence at-all?

A. No-sir, none.

Q. Now I-will-ask-your attention to William Broadhead.

A. He-filed his declaratory statement on-the 3d of Nov., 1868. There-are-no records of-his subsequent naturalization.

Contestant moves to-strike same-as-above.

Q. Is-this-the-gentleman known as Uncle Billy Broadhead, who-lives in-the poor-house?

A. The-name is-the-same, and-I-suppose it-is-the-same-man.

Q. Did-you-find that naturalization papers had-been issued to C. L. Petit-Demange?—if-so, give-the date.

A. On-the 22nd of June, 1882, he-filed his declaratory statement.

Contestant moves to-strike same-as-above.

Q. Then the-first papers are-all-that-you found to-have-been issued to-him?

A. Yes-sir.

Q. Did-you-find that-any-papers had-been issued to Frank Delaware?

A. No-sir, I-did-not.

Contestant moves to-strike same-as-above.

Q. I-will-ask-you if-you-have gone through these naturalization and-Court-records by-the index, or if-not, how did-you-examine them?

A. I-examined them both ways; first by index, and-then by-looking carefully over each page.

Q. State-whether-or-not you-found any record of-the naturalization of Edward Willigrod; if-so, what-is-the date of-it?

A. I-can state the-book and-the page from-memory. It-is-in Minute Book Number One, page fourteen, of-the records of-the County-Court. The-date is somewhere between 1856-58.

Contestant moves to-strike same-as-above.

Q. Does-the-record show-that two papers were issued?

A. No-sir, but-the record I-mention is-of-the issue of-the second, or official naturalization papers.

Q. What Court were-they issued from?

A. From-the County-Court, when Wm. C. Smith was judge. Contestant moves to-strike same-as-above.

Q. Mr. Johnson, you-say-you have examined these-records from-the beginning, page by page; will-you-please state more specifically as-to-what-records you-refer?

A. I-have examined Journals 1, 2 and 3, of-the Circuit-Court of Marshall-County, and-Journals A, B and C, of-the District-Court. The-remaining records form a-book called First Paper or Declaratory book. I-examined them all page by page.

Q. Are-there more-Journals than this in-the Circuit-Court?

A. Yes-sir.

Q. How-far does-the third Circuit-Court Journal extend?

A. Down-to 1873, when-the-first naturalization record was-begun.

Q. And-the District-Court Journal you-have referred-to covered the-same period?

A. Yes-sir.

Q. Mr. Johnson, will-you-please bring over-the-book containing the-record of-the papers issued to Mr. Willigrod?

Witness produces Naturalization Record-Book Number 2.

Q. Did-you-find this-book in-the office and-custody of-the clerk of-the District and-Circuit-Courts of-this-County?

A. Yes-sir, it-is-one of-the official records, kept in-the office of-the clerk whose deputy I-am.

Q. Please state-the title and-character of-the third book you-now have-in-your possession.

A. It-is called Minute-Book Number 1, of-the Marshall-County-Court, kept when Wm. C. Smith was judge.

Q. Please-turn-to page fourteen and-read the-record contained therein of-the naturalization of Mr. Willigrod.

Witness reads:

UNITED-STATES-OF-AMERICA, } ss.
STATE OF IOWA, MARSHALL-COUNTY.

Be-it remembered that-at-a-term of-the County-Court held in-and-for said-County, State of Iowa, on-the 26th day of-February, in-the year of-our Lord, 1856, was-present the-Honorable Wm. C. Smith, sole-presiding judge, and *ex-officio* clerk of-said Court, when-the following among-other proceedings were-had, to wit: Edward Willigrod, a-native of-Germany, and-at-present residing in-said State, appeared in-open Court and-made application to-be admitted to-become a-citizen of-the United-States, and-it appearing to-the satisfaction of-the Court that-he-had declared on-oath before-the-clerk of-the Marshall-County-Court, two years before-his admission, that-it-was *bona-fide* his-intention to-become a-citizen of-the United-States and-to renounce forever all allegiance to any-other Prince, Potentate, State or Sovereignty whatsoever, and-especially to-the King-of-Germany, to whom he-was heretofore a-subject; and-said applicant having declared on-oath before-this Court that-he will support the Constitution-of-the-United-States, and-that-he doth absolutely and-entirely abjure and-renounce all-allegiance to any foreign Prince, Potentate, State, or Sovereignty whatsoever, and-particularly to William, reigning King-of-Germany, to whom he-has hitherto been-a-subject.

(Signed) WM. C. SMITH, County Judge.

CROSS-EXAMINATION.

Q. What-is-your official-position in-this-county, Mr. Johnson?
A. I-am deputy County-Clerk.
Q. Are-you deputy County-Clerk, or deputy County Auditor?
A. I-am both at-present.
Q. When-were-you appointed deputy clerk?
A. On-the 10th of-April, '83.
Q. When-did-you-make-the-examination of-Court-records which-you-have referred-to?
A. Since receiving my appointment.
Q. You still retain your position in-the Auditor's office?
A. Yes-sir.
Q. How much time did-you spend in-making this examination?

PROFESSIONAL CONDUCT.   175

A. The-greater portion of-the day and-also most of-the evenings for-two-weeks.   Excused.

(14 m).

488.

FREDERICK
  vs.   } REBUTTING EVIDENCE ON PART OF CONTESTANT.
WILSON.

Jas. C. Cochran, sworn.

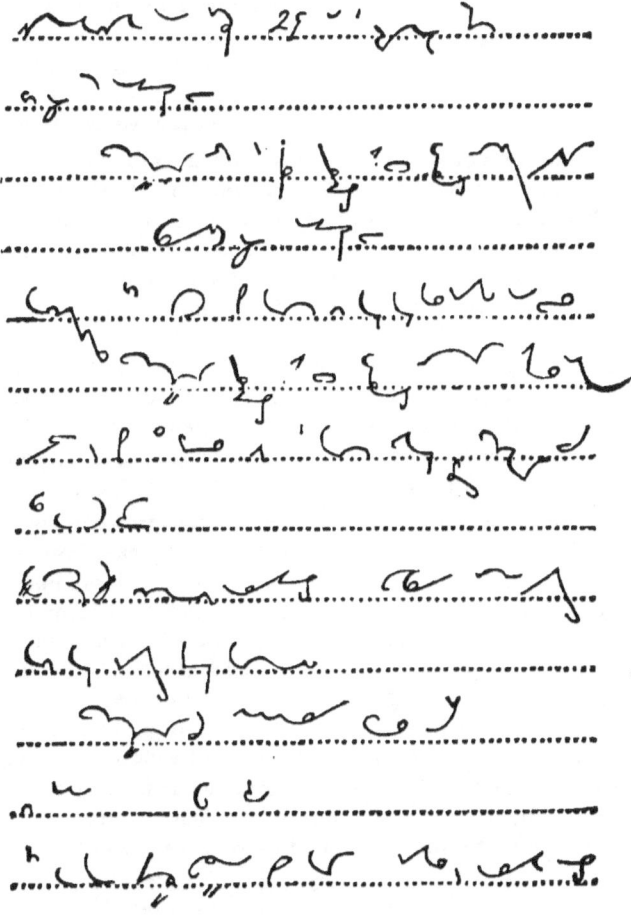

SUGGESTIONS.

"HAVE FAITH IN SHORT-HAND.—There is probably no other one thing that has caused so many people to fail in their endeavors to become reporters as a lack of confidence in Short-hand. Too often we hear beginners say. 'I will try it and see whether I can succeed or not.' The young man or woman who, after seeing that thousands of others have made a success of Short-hand, cannot say, 'I *will* succeed,' had better not spend time or money upon it, or, in fact, upon anything else that requires a little study and application.

"Nothing is more absurd than to hear a certain class of people decrying Short-hand, when in fact they know nothing at all about it. We have known many young people who would have become excellent reporters, had they not been induced to give up the idea of learning Short-hand by the advice of persons who had never before even heard of Stenography.

"The young man or woman who takes up the study of Short-hand will surely be compelled to endure the constant cry that there is an over-supply. To be sure there is an 'over-supply' of Short-hand writers. So is there an over-supply of workmen in every industrial pursuit; yet people go on learning the various trades just as though the cry had never been heard. The over-supply comes from that large class who only do things by halves. We have all heard the cry of an over-supply of lawyers, teachers, carpenters, blacksmiths, etc., yet a good lawyer, teacher or carpenter is never at a loss for something to do. You never hear of a man who stands well up in his business or profession making any complaint of the competition which he may have. People who can do their part well are always in demand."

"The Stenographer, like everybody else, must, in a certain sense, be a machine. This arises from the fact that in many cases confidential matter of the gravest importance is dictated to him, and unless he exerts the utmost care, he will be apt, inadvertently it may be, to betray a knowledge of his employer's affairs to those who would take advantage of it. Again, it frequently occurs in some kinds of business that the Stenographer is approached for the special purpose of getting him to divulge his employer's intentions or plans. Attempts may even be made to bribe him, in order to secure the desired information. Aside from the moral phase of the question, the Stenographer can by no means afford to betray his employer's secrets to others. Once let it be proved that he has done such a thing, and his prospects as a reporter will be ruined."

—*From* "ONE HUNDRED VALUABLE SUGGESTIONS TO SHORT-HAND STUDENTS," *by Selby A. Moran, Short-Hand Institute, Michigan University.*

Vocabulary of Word and Phrase Signs.

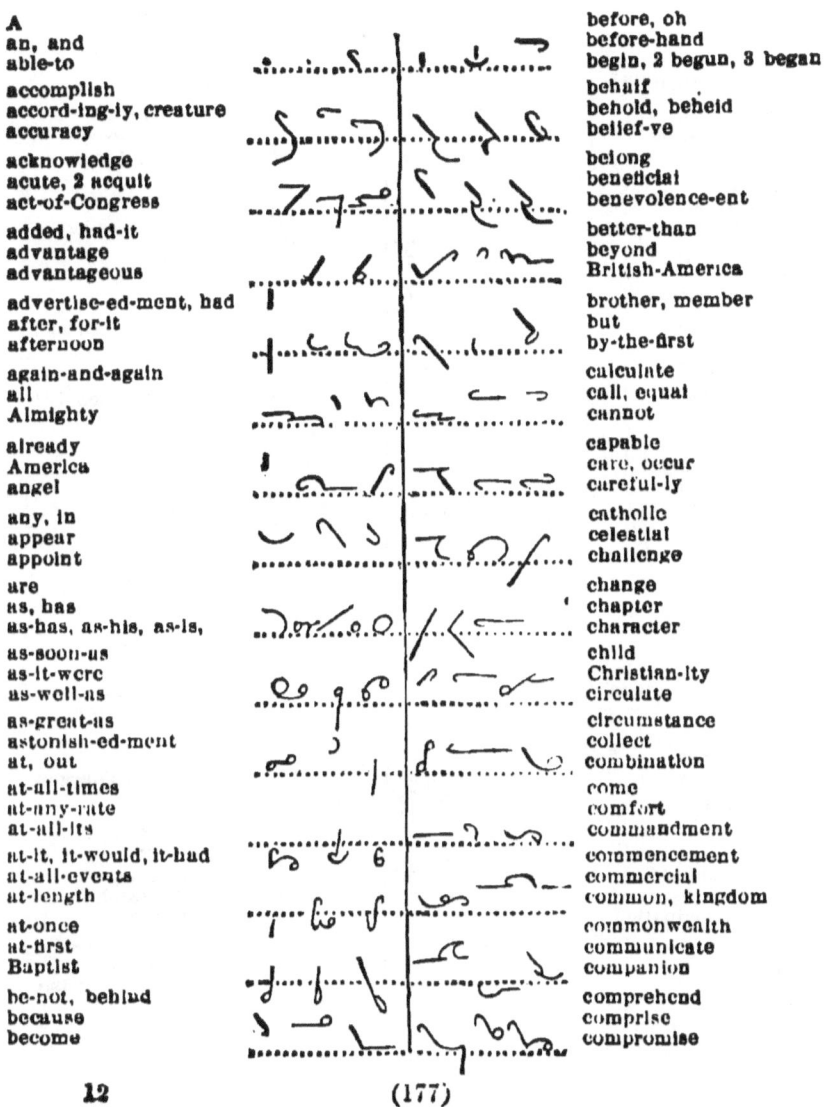

A
an, and
able-to
accomplish
accord-ing-ly, creature
accuracy
acknowledge
acute, 2 acquit
act-of-Congress
added, had-it
advantage
advantageous
advertise-ed-ed-ment, had
after, for-it
afternoon
again-and-again
all
Almighty
already
America
angel
any, in
appear
appoint
are
as, has
as-has, as-his, as-is,
as-soon-as
as-it-were
as-well-as
as-great-as
astonish-ed-ment
at, out
at-all-times
at-any-rate
at-all-its
at-it, it-would, it-had
at-all-events
at-length
at-once
at-first
Baptist
be-not, behind
because
become

before, oh
before-hand
begin, 2 begun, 3 began
behalf
behold, beheld
belief-ve
belong
beneficial
benevolence-ent
better-than
beyond
British-America
brother, member
but
by-the-first
calculate
call, equal
cannot
capable
care, occur
careful-ly
catholic
celestial
challenge
change
chapter
character
child
Christian-ity
circulate
circumstance
collect
combination
come
comfort
commandment
commencement
commercial
common, kingdom
commonwealth
communicate
companion
comprehend
comprise
compromise

VOCABULARY OF WORD AND PHRASE SIGNS.

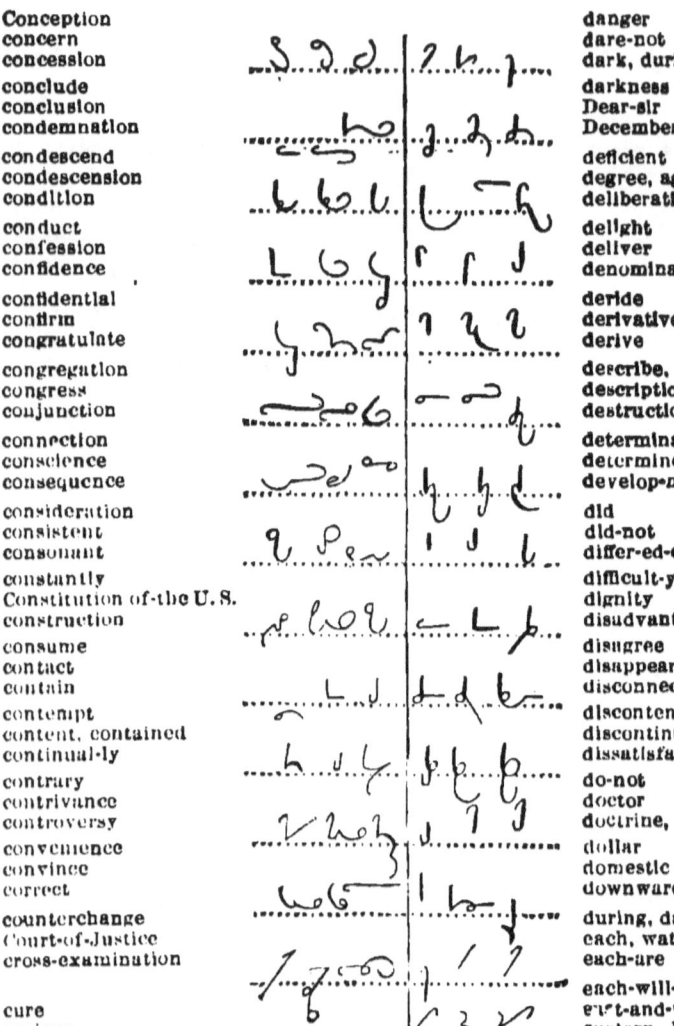

Conception	danger
concern	dare-not
concession	dark, during
conclude	darkness
conclusion	Dear-sir
condemnation	December
condescend	deficient
condescension	degree, agree
condition	deliberation
conduct	delight
confession	deliver
confidence	denominate-ion
confidential	deride
confirm	derivative
congratulate	derive
congregation	describe, scripture
congress	description
conjunction	destruction
connection	determination
conscience	determine
consequence	develop-ment
consideration	did
consistent	did-not
consonant	differ-ed-ence-ent
constantly	difficult-y
Constitution of-the U. S.	dignity
construction	disadvantage
consume	disagree
contact	disappear
contain	disconnect
contempt	discontent
content, contained	discontinue
continual-ly	dissatisfaction
contrary	do-not
contrivance	doctor
controversy	doctrine, 3 darken
convenience	dollar
convince	domestic
correct	downward
counterchange	during, dark
Court-of-Justice	each, watch
cross-examination	each-are
	each-will-have
cure	east-and-west
curious	eastern, historian

VOCABULARY OF WORD AND PHRASE SIGNS.

Efficient electric-ity emphatic	Gentleman, 1 gentlemen Gentlemen-of-the-Jury give
enlarge equal, call especial-ly	give-it glory-fy glorious
essential-ly establish-ed-ment eternal	good-and-bad govern-ed-ment Great-Britain
European ever-and-ever everlasting	greater-than great-extent guilt-y
every-one examination exchange	had, advertisement had-not half, few
expect experience explanation	hand hand-in-hand happen
expression extemporaneous external	happiness happy, hope hard, heard, word
extraordinary fact, future failure	hardware has, as have
faithful falsehood familiar	have-it have-not have-had
fear-of-God feature, if-it first	he health-y hear, her, here
follow for for-the-most-part	heart heaven height
for-instance forgive forsake, for-the-sake-of	help hence heretofore
forward from from-it, effort	hesitate high, I, eye highly
full function future, fact	highway, Iowa him his, is
gave-it general-ly generation	his-is, is-his, is-as history hold, held

VOCABULARY OF WORD AND PHRASE SIGNS.

Holiness	Indian-Territory
home	individual
honorable	infinite
hope, happy	influence
how	influential
however	information
howsoever	injunction
human-life	inquire-y, anywhere
humble	insignificance-ant
humor	intellect-ual
	intelligence
hundred	intelligent
I, eye, high	into, 3 unite
idea	invention
if, off	irregular
illegible	is, his
imagine	is-said
immediate-ly	is-safe
importance-ant	is-such
impossible	is-seen
improves-ments	island, I-will-not
inacurate	it-would-have, out-of
in-the-world	it-will-have, twelve
in-the-second-place	it-is-simply
in-regard-to	it-ought-not
in-point-of-fact	it-not
in-order-that	it-ought-to-have-had
in-seeming	it-will-not
in-his-usual	it-would-have-had
in-his-expression	it-would, it-bad
in-his-experience	it-ought-to-have
in-his-description	it-would-not, it-had-not
in-consideration	it-will-have-had
in-as-many	January
in-some	Jesus-Christ
in-his-situation	junior
in-respect-to	Justice-of-the-Peace
in-reference-to	just-had
in-order-to	kingdom-of-heaven
in-his-secret	knowledge
inclination	ladies-and-gentlemen
income	landlord
incompetent	language
inconsistent	large
inconvenience	larger-than

VOCABULARY OF WORD AND PHRASE SIGNS. 181

Lawyer
lead
legible

liberty-of-the-people
liberty-of-the-press
Lord

Lord-Jesus-Christ
loves-us
magazine, magnanimous

magnetism
majesty
majority

manner, 3 owner
manuscript
may-not

may-be, improvement
member, remember
member-of-Congress

member-of-the-bar
member-of-the-Leg.
merciful

minority
misconduct
mistake

more, mercy
more-than
mortgage

mostly, may-as-well
most-likely
Mr., remark-able

much
much-are
much-will-have

must-be
mystery
natural

neglect
negligent
neighborhood

never
New-York-City
New-Hampshire

next
nor, near, honor
North-America

North-western
notwithstanding
November

now
nowhere
number, brother

object
objective
objection

occur
of
of-it

on
on-the-other-hand
on-either-hand

on-the-one-hand
one
one-of-the-best

one-of-the-most
one-or-two
onward

opinion
opportunity
or

organize
organization
other, 1 either

ought
ought-to-have
our

our-own
out-of
over-and-over-again

overwhelm
part-y
partake

particular-ly
peculiar-ity
people

people-of-God
perfect
perfection

philanthropy
phonography
plaintiff

VOCABULARY OF WORD AND PHRASE SIGNS.

Pleasure	respectability
political	revelation
popular	revolution
posterity	rule, 2 roll
postmark	said-to-have
post-office	salvation
poverty	sanction
practicable	scripture, describe
practice-al	second
principle-al	secure
probable-ly	senior
profit, prophet	set-off, set-forth
proof, prove	several, Savior
proper-ty	shall
prosperity	short-hand
Providence	should
providential	signification
public-ish-ed	similar
punish-ed-ment	simple-ly
quality	so-much
question	some-one
quick	something
quiet	sometimes
railroad	somewhat
railway-car	South-America
rather-than	speak, speech
reality	special, spoke
real-ly, rely	spirit,
recollect	spoken
recompense	square
reconsider	strength
reduction	student
reform	subject
reformation	subjection
regular	substantial
reliable	such-a-one
religion	such-are
religious	such-were
relinquish	such-are-not
remark-able, Mr.	such-were-not
re-member	such-ought-to-have-had
represent	such-would-have-had
representation	sufficient
republic	suggestion
respect-able	surprise, 3 suppress

VOCABULARY OF WORD AND PHRASE SIGNS. 183

Takes-us temperance-ate temptation		usual-ly virtue was
territory Testament testimony		watch, each water we
thank, oath, youth that the		we-are we-are-not we-will, while
their, there, they-are them, they therefore		we-may we-may-be we-must
they-will they-are-not thing		welcome well, 3 awhile what
think this-is, themselves this-system		whatever when whensoever
those, thus though, thou three, 3 through		where, 3 aware wherefore which
to to-be together		which-ever, which, have which will-not which-would-have
too, two true truth		which-ought-not which-not which- w'd (or had) not
try-to-have twelve unaware		which-are which-are-not which-ought-to-have
uncommon unconscious under		which-were-not which-will-have while, we-will
understand union unite-y		white who whoever, who-have
United-States universal university		whole whom, home whose, use
unless until until-it		will will-not wisdom
upon-it upon-his us, use		wish, 3 issue with with-regard-to

VOCABULARY OF WORD AND PHRASE SIGNS.

With-him, I with-me with-reference-to with-respect-to within, heathen without witness word, heard Word-of-God world	worship would ye, year-s yesterday yet young young-man young-woman yourself.

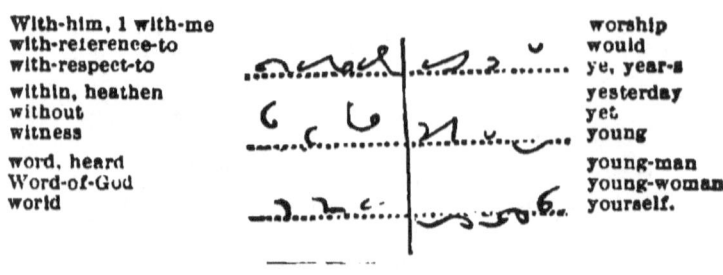

ADDENDA.

Children nevertheless.	will (noun) Yours-truly.

stenography phonographic single	is-it as-it herein
altogether value throughout	instruction instructive English- language
satisfactory satisfy south-eastern	just-as-much- as just-as-well-as in-the-first- place
was-there for-there may-there	whether have-there further-than

VERBATIM REPORTING SPEED.

It will be the wish of some, after completing the prescribed course, to continue the study with the view of gaining the speed necessary to record rapid speeches. Whether it is your intention or not to engage in verbatim reporting, the determination of reaching the highest degree of skill you are able, is commendable. Your fitness for success in the higher branches of the stenographic profession can be decided upon when you have finished the principles. To furnish a few explicit rules to guide you in pursuing an advanced course is the object of these paragraphs. A few months' service as short-hand amanuensis, especially if a situation as assistant to a professional stenographer can be secured, is recommended as a very valuable means to the end sought.

As matter for dictation you should select newspaper articles, sermons, speeches, reports of law-suits, and the proceedings of legislatures and conventions; also biographies, histories, or any publication in which the ordinary phraseology of public or private discourse is employed. Volumes of business letters, and law and association reports printed from stenographic notes, have been published for the use of advanced students. Copies may be had by applying to the Reporters' Bureau.

Your dictation practice should be daily and systematic. The person who reads should be instructed to pronounce the sentences after the manner of public speakers, and not slowly drawl out the words to suit your pen. A pause at the end of a clause or sentence may be made for your benefit. In this way the power will be cultivated of recollecting long sentences until you have written them. This kind of memory, called verbal, is altogether indispensible to the verbatim reporter. Not only can the stenographer more easily follow a public speaker by keeping several words behind him, but, since public orators often, when least expected, deliver two or three sentences in rapid succession, memory as well as speed is needed by the reporter.

At this point you may try your hand at taking down public lectures, sermons, etc., selecting of course the most deliberate speakers. It will not be possible to get every word at first. The proper course is to write whole sentences rather than merely words here and there as they may be caught. The notes thus taken should be read afterwards, and occasionally a carefully written transcript ought to be made, correctly spelled and punctuated. Pen and ink should be used, and a writing table provided whenever practicable.

One cannot condemn too severely the habit of some misguided students of practicing upon speakers so fluent that efforts to follow are all in vain, getting the heads of some sentences only and the tails of others, in hieroglyphics so deformed as to be utterly undecipherable.

The reporting of speeches may be supplemented by occasional practice in taking down the testimony of witnesses, and the other proceedings had in trials at court, before magistrates, or the evidence given before notaries. The form of report made use of in law-suits may be employed also in taking down conversations.

A good plan is now and then to take letters and other papers for the accommodation of persons who will afterwards examine and criticise your transcripts. During this period a frequent correspondence in short-hand with other students equally advanced will prove valuable. It will be a serious mistake if you seek to go over a great deal of ground at the expense of thoroughness of work. Leave no selection until you have written it half a dozen times and read it over at least twice.

The Reporting Style of Short-Hand.

The very latest and most improved text-book of stenography. The Reporting Style of the American Pitman System is taught, the method now employed by nine-tenths of the professional reporters. The subject is so clearly and logically presented that no one can fail to understand it. This work unquestionably possesses the following points of superiority:

1. The Corresponding Style is discarded, which greatly facilitates the acquirement of the art.
2. The learner is instructed how to execute the characters rapidly, and given such assistance as will enable him to become *practically efficient*.
3. No word is introduced until every principle has been explained upon which the formation of its most approved outline depends.
4. The course of instruction is distinctively progressive, and every lesson accompanied with appropriate reading and writing exercises.
5. Word and phrase signs are introduced early in the course.
6. A series of lessons are added on professional reporting, such as are found in *no other text-book whatever*.

COMMENDATIONS.

THE "REPORTING STYLE."

A thoroughly practical instruction book.—HOME AND SCHOOL VISITOR, Greenfield, Ind.

This is a brief, simple and satisfactory treatise.—SCHOOL BULLETIN, Syracuse, New York.

In many respects the best work on Phonography that has appeared for several years.—D. P. LINDSLEY, Inventor of Takigraphy.

A complete and systematic treatise on Stenography and the reporting business.—THE TEACHER, Philadelphia, Pa.

Contains all that is of value in qualifying the learner for practical reporting.—THE NORMAL TEACHER, Danville, Ind.

This book teaches the Pitman style of reporting direct, discarding the corresponding style. It is a brief, simple and satisfactory treatise.—STATE EDUCATIONAL JOURNAL, Syracuse, N. Y.

A systematic series of lessons that will no doubt prove very acceptable to both instructors and pupils as a text-book, and will be found particularly useful to those who are undergoing a course of self-instruction.—CHICAGO EVENING JOURNAL.

The character of the work is aptly described by its title, and it possesses the great merit of clearly presenting the reporting style of the American Pitman System, divested of that useless appendage, the Corresponding Style, so-called.

University School of Short-Hand.

Full course given in the Reporting Style. Young ladies and gentlemen prepared for secretaryships in four months. Sessions continue throughout the year. Pupils may enter at any time. The various kinds of Type-writers are taught by an experienced operator. No assistants employed who are not practical reporters.

A few of its graduates are referred to: W. A. Shepfer, with Yanz, Griggs & Howes, St. Paul, Minn.; Alberto A. Ladd, with Gen'l Mngr. C. M. & St. P. Ry., Milwaukee, Wis.; Marion Grayson, with the Conn. Ins. Co., Hartford, Conn.; Isaac W. Bennett, Instructor, Walla Walla, Wash. Ter.; Coralie S. Roth, with Singer Mnfg. Co., New Orleans, La.; Bessie Gardner, with Fire and Marine Ins. Co., St. Paul, Minn.; Ralph W. Miller, Stenographer, Kansas City, Mo.; Agnes Lord, with the "School of Expression," Boston, Mass.; Noyes W. Willet, Court Reporter, Rapid City, Dak.; Mira E. Morgan, Stenographer, Santa Barbara, Cal.; J. G. Dixon, Court Reporter, Boulder, Col; Ed. W. Dobson, with Childers & Fergusson, Albuquerque, N. M.; Jno. M. Lackey, Court Reporter, Montgomery, Ala.; Horace L. Winslow, Stenographic Instructor, Newton, Iowa.

TERMS:

Full Course in Stenography at the School	$40 00
Full Course by Mail, Fifty Lessons	20 00
Type-writer Instruction by Mail, or at the School	10 00
Orthography, Full Course by Mail	5 00

THE REPORTERS' BUREAU

Assists graduates in obtaining situations. The Manager is often able to secure a position in whatever location the student wishes to live. This Bureau was established for the sole *purpose* of assisting the students *whom we ourselves instruct*, and for whose qualifications we can vouch. Since we present the names of our own students only, whose skill we are able to certify to, business men give credit to our recommendations, and often **employ our graduates outright**, without the usual preliminary trial month.

Over four hundred young men and women who have graduated from the School of Short-Hand are now occupying lucrative situations in all the principal cities.

Perfected Method of Postal Instruction.

The most thorough plan ever contrived of teaching Short-hand by mail. Some of the features which recommend it are:

1. A system of writing can be taught by mail far more successfully than any other art or science.

2. The student runs no risk—is not obliged to leave home or give up his business.

PERFECTED METHOD OF POSTAL INSTRUCTION.

3. Lessons are received at whatever intervals are most convenient.
4. Corrected exercises are invariably sent back by return mail.
5. Lessons are carried in the pocket and learned at leisure moments.
6. Traveling does not interfere in the least with this method of teaching.
7. Short-hand is best learned by devoting to it only a fraction of one's time daily, a plan suited to the convenience of busy people, who have most occasion to use a brief system of writing.
8. Students are required to write and read the exercises with gradually increased speed. This is the only certain way of gaining proficiency in a short space of time.
9. Not only is the art thoroughly taught, but full directions are given as to its use in the business of Amanuensis, Court, and Legislative reporting, etc.
10. The intelligent student can as certainly learn by this means as by attending college, and with but a fraction of the expense.
11. By the use of a series of Circulators, students communicate with each other, become acquainted, and a friendly competition is established.
12. Lessons may be received daily, although the student lives thousands of miles distant.
13. A full course in Orthography is also given by mail for the accommodation of those who wish to perfect themselves in this branch.
14. The use of the Type-writer, the usual accompaniment of short-hand, is also taught by mail.
15. Local Classes are formed, and meet for practice every week under the direction of a competent drill-master.

TESTIMONIALS.

I have mastered short-hand in six months, taking lessons by mail. I have thus acquired a paying business at leisure hours that would otherwise have been wasted.—W. H. Jenkins, Swan Lake, Ia.

While trying to learn by means of self-instruction, I went astray a thousand times. I find this method entirely satisfactory, and especially serviceable to me, as I am allowed to receive lessons slowly at times when pressed with other work.—Rev. W. C. Madison, Grand Junction, Col.

I do not see how it would be possible to make the Course more complete or interesting. I find the lessons entirely satisfactory, and sincerely believe that any person can become a proficient stenographer by this means, if he is capable of learning at all.—T. J. Rollman, Superintendent Public Schools, Brookville, Kansas.

By means of this plan I have been able to learn short-hand, devoting to it only my leisure moments. I cannot recommend it too highly.—Hattie Lewis, Stenographer to the Homestead Pub. Co., Des Moines, Ia.

I can now write very rapidly, and what is equally important, *read* what is written. I learned entirely by mail, and at a trifling expense. Prof. Moran's scheme of postal instruction is simply unparalleled—nothing could be better. I have examined various text books, but his instruction book on the Reporting Style, which is the basis of this plan, is the most free from useless matter, clearest, the most concise, and best arranged of all.—Cyrus W. Phelps, Stenographer, Marshalltown, Iowa.

TRIAL LESSON FREE.

THE NEW ENGLAND
SHORT-HAND AND TYPE-WRITING SCHOOL.

ALSO

GENERAL STENOGRAPHIC AND TYPE-WRITING SUPPLY AGENCY.

S. G. GREENWOOD, Principal.

INSTRUCTION BY MAIL A SPECIALTY.

TRIAL LESSONS FREE.

PERIODICALS.—All the leading Magizines, both domestic and foreign. Sample copies furnished and subscriptions solicited.

TEXT-BOOKS.—Our stock contains the text-books of all the standard Short-hand systems, both foreign and domestic.

TYPE-WRITER SUPPLIES.—We have in stock at all times a complete line of Type-writer Paper, Ribbons, Carbons, Instruction Books, etc. Samples furnished if desired.

TYPE-WRITER MACHINES.—We buy, sell and rent any of the standard Machines in any part of the United States.

STENOGRAPHER'S SUPPLIES.—This department, we claim, is as full and complete as any in the world, and we are constantly adding to it, having standing orders with all the Publishers and Manufactories in this country and Europe. Nothing new escapes us.

GENERAL SUPPLIES.—We also carry in stock a large assortment of new and interesting books on self-help and home culture, as well as a full line of Stationery, also Office and Library Furniture in a large variety.

Send two cent stamp for Illustrated Cotalogue. Remit by postal note or money order.

Address **S. G. GREENWOOD,**
33 Pemberton Sq., Boston, Mass.

NATIONAL SYSTEM
Co-Operative Schools of Short-Hand.

THE FOLLOWING SCHOOLS ARE RECOMMENDED AS WELL EQUIPPED CORRESPONDENCE SCHOOLS, MAKING USE OF THE PERFECTED POSTAL METHOD, PATENTED BY ELDON MORAN.

McGILVRA COLLEGE OF SHORT-HAND,
McGilvra Bros., Proprietors, Richmond, Va.

SCHOOL OF SHORT-HAND,
Isaac W. Bennett, Principal, Walla Walla, Washington Ter.

THE EXCELSIOR COLLEGE,
Wilmot & Moore, Proprietors, Milwaukee, Wis.

THE IOWA CITY SCHOOL OF SHORT-HAND,
Geo. S. Forest, Principal, Iowa City, Iowa.

THE NEW ENGLAND SCHOOL OF SHORT-HAND,
S. G. Greenwood, Principal, 33 Pemberton Sq., Boston, Mass.

THE INDIANAPOLIS SCHOOL OF SHORT-HAND,
J. A. Duthie, Principal, Vance Block, Indianapolis, Ind.

SCHOOL OF SHORT-HAND,
Jno. H. Goldman, Principal, Columbia, Mo.

CORRESPONDENCE SCHOOL,
J. G. Dixon, Principal, Manhattan, Kansas.

THE OHIO SCHOOL OF SHORT-HAND,
Geo. Fritz, Principal, Ottawa, Ohio.

THE NEW JERSEY SCHOOL OF SHORT-HAND,
H. W. Smith, Principal, 103 Ward Street, Patterson, N. J.

Stenographic Supply Agency,

IOWA CITY, IOWA.

Depot for Short-Hand and Type-Writer Students' Material and General Stenographic and Reporters' Supplies.

The ELDON MORAN Series of Short-Hand Works:

THE REPORTING STYLE OF SHORT-HAND.

Price, $1.50. The latest and most complete Text-book of American Phonography. Fifth edition now selling. Revised edition in preparation. This is the most popular text-book for self-instruction of any published.

THE SIGN-BOOK.

Price, 25cts. A vest-pocket manual of all the abbreviations, word and phrase signs used in the Pitman System, designed as an accompaniment of the "Reporting Style."

THE MANUAL OF POSTAL INSTRUCTION.

Price, 25cts. A complete guide of Correspondence Teaching. It should be in the hands of every person who intends to learn Short-hand, Type-writing or Orthography by mail. Third edition.

TEST-LESSON BOOK.

Twenty-four pages, price, 2cts. The test-lessons are so arranged and the necessary tests so applied in this ingenious little book, that any person may, by means of it, determine accurately the degree of fitness or aptitude they naturally possess for success in the business of Short-hand and Type-writing. Twenty-three editions of this little work have already been published. All persons interested in Short-hand should procure a copy without delay.

100 VALUABLE SUGGESTIONS TO SHORT-HAND STUDENTS.

By Selby A. Moran, Principal Stenographic Institute, Ann Arbor, Mich. Price, $1.00. The degree of popularity with which this book has been received is indicated by the fact that one thousand copies were sold within the first year. It is a guide to the Reporting Business, the matter being arranged in the form of a dictation book; so it is valuable for both teacher and pupil.

STUDENTS' PRACTICE TABLETS.—2 for 25cts.

REPORTERS' NOTE BOOK.—Price 25cts.

THE UNION READING CIRCLE.

Subscription per year, $1.00. A Literary Journal. Stenographic Department edited by Eldon Moran. Sample copies, 10cts.

Agents wanted everywhere. Liberal discount to teachers. Information furnished upon application. Address all orders to

STENOGRAPHIC SUPPLY AGENCY, Iowa City, Iowa.

www.ingramcontent.com/pod-product-compliance
Lightning Source LLC
Chambersburg PA
CBHW032138160426
43197CB00008B/699